WITHDRAWN

KENNETH E. BOULDING

A PRIMER ON SOCIAL DYNAMICS

HISTORY AS DIALECTICS AND DEVELOPMENT

THE FREE PRESS · NEW YORK
COLLIER-MACMILLAN LIMITED · LONDON

THE FREE PRESS
A Division of The Macmillan Company
866 Third Avenue, New York, New York 10022

Collier-Macmillan Ltd., Toronto, Ontario

Library of Congress Catalog Card Number: 70–123192
printing number
2 3 4 5 6 7 8 9 10

PREFACE

The thesis of this book is that there are two major types of processes at work in human history and in the dynamics of society. On the one hand there are dialectical processes. These involve conflict and the victory of one group or system over another, and hence a succession of victors. On the other hand there are nondialectical (or developmental) processes in which conflict, even where it exists, is incidental, and in which the central pattern of the process is cumulative, evolutionary, and continuous. My main proposition is that the dialectical processes—important as they are in the short run, and significant as they are to those participating in them—are not the major processes of history but only waves and turbulences on the great historical tides of evolution and development, which themselves are fundamentally nondialectical.

This view, of course, runs counter to a number of widely

held and popular interpretations of history. It is rather obvious that dialectical views of history, whether at the popular or at the philosophical level, have predominated. People have always looked at history as the struggle of "us" against "them." It is not surprising that short-term views predominate, because we all live *in* the short run, and it is *in* the short run that the dialectics of nation, class, race, party, and faction tend to form the human horizon. It is also not surprising, therefore, that philosophers and thinkers have arisen to justify "us" in the conflict against "them." In spite of all this, I am convinced that there is a larger horizon, and that we must therefore look beyond dialectics and toward development.

This book is quite frankly polemical. It is a tract rather than a treatise, a work of reflection rather than of scholarship; and at the same time it is intended to give the reader at least an outline of a general developmental theory of social dynamics and of human history, which only the future can develop in detail. The polemic is directed particularly against what I call "dialectical philosophy," which I define as "all those ideologies which regard conflict as the essential process in development and therefore tend to put a high intrinsic value on conflict, struggle, war, and revolution."

I am not arguing that all dialectical processes are bad, but I do think they have a bias in that direction which is enhanced by the presence of the dialectical philosophy or ideology. It is in societies where the prevailing ideologies are nondialectical—stressing community, agreement, orderliness, courtesy, and love, rather than conflict, turbulence, confrontation, envy, and hate—that the dialectical processes themselves are likely to be most fruitful. A dialectical philosophy, however, whether nationalistic, racist, or Marxist, which stresses victory rather than problem-solving, beating down the enemy rather than cooperating with him (and which therefore tends to justify and excuse the immoral behavior which dialectical processes always produce), is likely to intensify the dialectical processes themselves to the point where they will become damaging to all parties, and unfriendly to human welfare and development.

I will not be surprised if the Marxists feel that I am unfair to Marx and to them. Indeed, I may be accused of engaging in precisely the dialectical processes of which I am so suspicious, for a polemical book is inevitably part of a dialectical process. But be this as it may, it is unfair to put nationalism, racism, and Marxism in the same stable of dialectical philosophy. The appropriate word here would be "classism," but the word does not seem to exist, and "Marxism" has become a synonym for it. The moral strength of Marxism is its sympathy with the oppressed, which is much more compatible with the class dialectic than with the dialectic of nation or race. Furthermore, Marx himself was a towering figure with a prophetic moral challenge which demands a response of some kind. When great men are wrong, however, they do all the more damage. It is when error is bound up with truth, and evil with good, that error and evil achieve power. While morally, therefore, Marx is a far superior figure to (shall we say) a Hitler or a Napoleon, as charismatic legitimators of dialectical processes they wear the same brand: all three have created an immense amount of human misery.

The development of a theory of social dynamics which is accurate enough so that it does not lead men into the justification of disastrous courses is a moral task of first importance. This a task which neither I nor any other individual has the capacity to carry out under his own power. This book is, in a manner of speaking, only one little brick contributed to the house which mankind one day must build to live in. If it encourages others to engage in the same task, it will have fulfilled its purpose.

The origins of this book in my own thinking go back a

good many years. As a young man I rejected both the bloody dialectic of nationalism which produced the First World War, and the no less fierce dialectic of communism which exterminated the Kulaks. I was influenced more perhaps than I then realized by the broad social dynamics of Schumpeter, with whom I studied briefly. From pure economics I graduated into general social dynamics, largely as a result of studying the labor movement. In the course of developing a general theory of conflict at the Center for Research on Conflict Resolution at the University of Michigan, I developed the idea of society as a threefold, genetic, evolutionary process involving the social "genes" of threat, exchange, and integrative relationships. My year at the University College of the West Indies in Jamaica (1959–60) was particularly helpful in this regard. The present work, however, owes its origin mainly to the year I spent in Japan at the International Christian University in Mitaka at Tokyo (1963–64). I was greatly stimulated and challenged by my students, many of whom were Marxists; and the lectures which formed the first draft of this volume were given largely in response to that stimulation.

The Case Study on Japan which I append to this volume is in part a reflection of that stimulation, and a small tribute to what was perhaps the most exciting year of my life. I hope it may be the beginning of a whole series of case studies by those who are better qualified to do them than I, which will apply the principles of this essay to other times and places.

K. E. B.
Boulder, Colorado
February 1970

CONTENTS

CHAPTER 1
HISTORY AS SYSTEM

he very concept of an interpretation of history implies that processes in time, especially those concerned with man and society, have a degree of systematic pattern and behavior. What we mean by the interpretation of history is the perception and knowledge of the systematic patterns which exist in these processes. The validity of such knowledge is tested by its ability to generate two powers; first, the power of understanding the past, and second, the power of predicting the future. The first of these may be purely subjective. We may, for instance, have a belief that we understand the past, which is very satisfying to us. The pleasure we take in this belief is no guarantee of the accuracy of our understanding, even though a subjective belief that we do (or do not) understand the past is an important element in present behavior and in the present dynamics of any social system. The ability to predict is much harder to achieve than the ability to understand. There are indeed sharp limits on this ability which we may never overcome, for history is not a totally predictable system. Nevertheless, we do not have to insist on 100 percent accuracy in prediction. If we can improve the probability of our forecasts and be right a greater proportion of the time, this itself is a sign of advancing knowledge. We may distinguish four kinds of processes in time, and human history participates in all four.

Random process

We have, first, the *random process* such as the throwing of dice. The essence of this process is its unpredictability. This unpredictability depends on the fact that the recorded information about the process is irrelevant to its future course. We do not have to answer the philosophical question whether randomness is simply a deficiency in our knowledge or whether it is an essential principle of the real world, that is, whether we do not know something that in theory might be known or whether there is a process which is in principle unknowable. It is sufficient to define a random process as one in which what is known and recorded about it does not increase the probability with which we can predict the future. Thus, if we throw a series of dice and record the numbers—shall we say, six, two, three, one, six, five—then if this is a truly random series, the record up to any point offers us no clue whatever as to the next number. This does not deny the possibility that if we know all about the mechanics of the dice thrower, we might be able to predict the next number, but this mechanics is not included in the information which we have. Human history is full of these random elements and contains many events which could not possibly be predicted from the record of preceding events. This fact imposes a necessary limit on our ability to predict the historical future, though it does not mean that our ability to predict is zero, because there are also nonrandom elements in history.

Determined mechanical process

The second kind of process in time might be called the *determined mechanical dynamic process*. This is characterized by the property that the record of a limited number of events in the process enables us to predict the next event, and all subsequent events, with complete accuracy. Suppose, for instance, we have a process which consists of writing down the numbers zero, one, two, three, four, and five. We perceive immediately that there is an order, that each figure is greater by one than its predecessor. We can move from understanding into prediction by predicting that the next number will be six. Here, however, we encounter a fundamental principle. Understanding only leads to prediction if the system that we understand remains stable. If another person is writing down the above numbers, he may very well write down the number seven instead of six because up to number five he has followed one law, but beyond that he follows another. It is even possible that the first numbers might have been random.

Sometimes the failure of one law or of a limited understanding to predict results in the discovery of more general laws and wider understanding. The scientist has great faith that the fundamental processes in nature do not change suddenly, and hence we can always go on to deeper understanding and more accurate prediction. Where truly random processes are involved, however, this faith may not be justified, and in social systems there is great doubt whether we can ever wholly eliminate the random elements.

In mathematical terms, a numerical process in time is a *sequence,* or rather a special case of a sequence, for sequences can also occur in space. What we mean by *understanding* is the discovery of a difference or differential equation of finite degree which governs the sequence. A difference equation of the first degree is a stable relationship between any member of a sequence and the next member, as in the example above. In a difference equation of the second degree, the stable relationship is between *two* successive numbers of a sequence and the one following. Suppose, for instance, we write down the famous mathematical sequence 1, 1, 2, 3, 5, 8, 13, 21. A little observation reveals that each number is the sum of the two previous ones. (This is the Fibonacci series.) It is easy to predict that the next number in the series will be 34, and a little simple arithmetic enables us to continue the series as far as we wish.

The best example of such a determined mechanical dynamic process in history is the movement of the solar system, at least before the advent of artificial satellites and political astronomy. Complex as they are, the movements of the solar system can all be described by difference or differential equations of the second or third degree, and hence prediction can be made with astonishing accuracy. Astronomers, for instance, can predict the time of an eclipse within a second or less many years in the future. Even here we must add the caution that prediction depends on the continuance of the existing system. If, for instance, a large new body swept into the solar system, or if the sun became unstable, predictions based on the existing system would break down.

In human history, predictions and systems of this kind are very rare. Indeed, they are virtually confined to those cyclical elements in human experience which themselves depend on the cycles of the solar system, such as the day, the lunar month, and the solar year. It may be that phenomena such as the ice ages, which have played a great part even in human events, are of this determined mechanical dynamic nature, but up to now we understand so little about them that we cannot make any secure predictions. Generally speaking, the higher the degree and the more complex these processes, the harder it is to discover the law which governs them, that is, the harder it is to understand them.

The processes of social systems which best correspond to determined mechanical dynamic processes are processes which involve simple growth. Growth at a constant rate can be represented by a simple difference equation of the first degree, such as $x_{t+1} = Kx_t$, for each term in the sequence is a constant proportion of the term before it. Thus, if we leave money in an account growing at compound interest, as long as the rate of interest, that is, its rate of growth, remains constant, the principle sum is highly predictable at any future date into which the system extends. Suppose, for instance, the sum is initially $100 and doubles every 10 years. Then in 10 years it will be $200, in 20 years $400, in 30 years $800, and so on indefinitely into the future. Similarly, where a country is undergoing steady economic growth at a reasonably constant rate, we can again predict its growth into the future with some confidence. More complex use of systems of this kind might include a model which would relate the rate of growth in some simple way to the existing size of whatever it is that is growing. There is a good deal of evidence, for instance, for the proposition that, for those countries which are having a successful growth pattern, the rate of growth diminishes as the country gets richer. If this is a reasonably stable relationship, however, we can still make predictions with some confidence.

Mechanical dynamic processes have also been used with modest success in population projections. Here the basic relationship is that all people who are x years old today will either be $x + 1$ years old, or dead, in a year's time. If we can add to this some knowledge of the specific future death and birth rates in different age groups, we can project populations indefinitely into the future. Projections, however, must be distinguished sharply from predictions. A projection is what the future would be like if the system remained unchanged. Population projections have not been very successful as predictions simply because population systems have been subject to what are called parametric changes in the basic constants of the models on which the predictions are based. Thus, there have been at times sudden and unpredictable changes in birth rates, such as happened in many western countries around 1947 when birth rates rose sharply. Similarly there may be sudden changes in death rates, like the sharp fall in death rates in many tropical countries after 1950, due largely to the eradication of malaria. All dynamic social systems seem to be subject to unpredictable change, and hence the future very rarely follows a projected course.

Teleological process

There is a third type of process in time which is characteristic of human history, though it is not unknown in the animal kingdom, which might be called the *teleological* process. This is a process in which the movement through time is guided by some image or information structure which is expected to be realized at the end of a process but which already exists in the image or the information system of the actors in the system at the beginning. One of the best examples of such process is the construction of a building following an architect's blueprint. The exact form of the building is aready present in the information content of the blueprints; the process of building is constantly guided by this information in the sense that divergences from the blueprint are perceived and corrected as the process goes on. The characteristic operation of a teleological process, therefore, is that of correcting divergence between some realistic image of the existing state of affairs and some end or ideal which is conceived as the objective of the process.

The biological process of growth has something of this character. In the fertilized egg or seed, there is an information system in the genes which has some parallel to the blueprint. This information operates as a highly selective process, rejecting those events which do not lead towards the end of producing the phenotype and selecting those which do, just as the builder rejects events which do not lead towards the building as envisaged in the blueprint and selects those which do.

Prediction and understanding here are qualitatively different from what they are in the case of the mechanical dynamic processes. They consist essentially in knowing the blueprint which describes the end of the process and knowing also the selective power of the blueprint, that is, its ability to select those processes which will, in fact, lead to the envisioned end. The builder may have a blueprint but may be unable to build for lack of some essential materials. Similarly, the genes cannot build the body if it does not have the food and an appropriate environment. Knowing the blueprint and knowing the environment, however, we can make predictions of the end with some accuracy, always assuming that the system does not change. We predict, for instance, that a kitten will grow up into a cat, not into a dog, and that a grain of wheat will grow up into a wheat plant, not into an oak tree. These predictions, like all predictions, may be disappointed if the kitten or the seed is killed in infancy, but then, of course, the system has changed. Most teleological processes have some random elements in them. No two houses are exactly alike even when they have been built from the same blueprints, and we are never sure exactly what kind of a cat the kitten will turn into.

In human history and in social processes, the best examples of teleological processes are to be found in the carrying out of plans. Many countries have five-year plans for economic development. Similarly, a business firm plans an investment program; a student plans his college career. When a student enters a college, we can predict with a fair degree of accuracy that he will become a sophomore, a junior, a senior, and eventually will graduate. In the social system, however, these predictions are never 100 percent accurate, not only because the systems and goals may change but because the systems and goals contain random elements. Five-year plans may not be fulfilled, the firm with the best plans may go bankrupt, the student may fail his course or may decide to drop out.

Success in carrying out plans is an indication of the realism, or accuracy of the understanding, of the subjective social system on which the plan was based. If there are no random elements in the system, then the failure of prediction is a clear indication that something was wrong with the original understanding. The success of prediction is not absolute proof that the original understanding was correct, for it is possible in some cases for false understanding to give rise to true prediction with a certain probability. Where there are random elements in the system, even if the prediction fails, it does not mean that the understanding was necessarily wrong, for the prediction always has to be in terms of certain probability of something happening, which means that there is always some probability of the prediction not being fulfilled.

The existence of random elements in the system, or more accurately random elements in our understanding of the system, creates great difficulties for the process of increasing knowledge, that is, for human learning. If we make a prediction which we believe has 100 percent chance of coming true, then if it does not come true, we are almost bound to learn something. Indeed, disappointment, that is, the failure of predictions, is an essential element in human learning of all kinds, even though what we learn from it may not always be "true." Thus, if a student, who had been extremely confident that he was going to pass an examination, finds out that he has failed, he is forced to revise his image of the world. He may decide that he has not studied hard enough or that the examiners were incompetent. Unfortunately, the mere fact of failure is not sufficient to distinguish between these two inferences, and he will need to get further information. Nevertheless, his disappointment will force him to change his image of the world. Since learning involves a change in our image of the world, unless our image changes, we have no possibility of learning.

Suppose now that the student predicts that he has a fifty-fifty chance of passing the examination. No matter what happens, his prediction is fulfilled, and he will not be surprised. Unless, therefore, our image of the world is such that we can make predictions with a greater degree of probability than fifty percent, we will not be able to learn anything. Thus, the very possibility of knowledge involves eliminating random elements, at least up to the point where predictions can be made with a reasonably high degree of probability. In social systems, we often do this by reducing the degree of randomness in the system through some kind of organization. As we have observed, we cannot predict anything about the behavior of completely fair dice. If the dice are loaded, our capacity to predict their behavior is improved, and from observing the behavior we can find out something about the nature of the loading. A great deal of development, both in the biological and in the social world, can be thought of as "loading the dice" through creating organization. Thus, the interior temperature of a warm-blooded animal or of a thermostatically controlled house is much more predictable than the temperature of its immediate environment, simply because there is an organization to offset the random changes. Similarly, in economic life the fluctuation of a perfectly free market may be quite random and unpredictable. If, however, a price is pegged by some authority, such as the price of gold or of foreign exchange, its future is predictable as long as the pegging organization continues.

The evolutionary process: ecological systems

The fourth type of process through time we may call the *evolutionary process*. This has something in common with the teleological process in that it involves a process of selecting one out of a number of possible changes. The selective process, however, might be described as ecological rather than teleological. In building a house, the builder selects those materials and actions which conform to an original plan. In an evolutionary process, whether an original plan exists or not, such a plan is *neither* part of the information system *nor* a part of the process by which change takes place. Rather, the selective process is one which follows from the dynamics of population change in interacting populations. An ecological equilibrium, such as we may approximate in a pond, field, or forest, is an equilibrium of populations of different kinds of interacting species, populations which include populations of molecules and compounds in air, soil, and water, as well as populations of living things.

Ecological mutation consists essentially in the introduction of a population of a new species into a previous system of interacting populations. If there is a new equilibrium (and a feasible dynamic course toward it) which includes the new species, it will survive. If there is not such an equilibrium, the new species will disappear. The vast majority of mutations do not survive, but occasionally, a mutation arises which has survival power in the sense that a new ecological system can be established which includes it. This new system may also exclude other populations, so some old species may disappear. This is known as *ecological succession*. It is convenient analytically to break this down into a succession of ecological equilibrium states, though, in fact, the processes of change are apt to be continuous and are neither more nor less than what we mean by evolution. This succession of ecological states might take place either by a change in physical conditions, such as the gradual filling up of a pond or a drying out of a desert, or through genetic mutation, producing new living species and displacing old ones.

The mechanism of ecological equilibrium, succession, and evolutionary change is always through the dynamics of population change of particular species. The population of any species will increase if the number of births exceeds the number of deaths. It will be stable, that is, in dynamic equilibrium, if the number of births is equal to the number of deaths. It will decline if the number of deaths exceeds the number of births. The number of births and deaths in a given species in a given time is related to its environment, that is, to the populations of species which surround it and with which it interacts. These relationships may be either competitive or cooperative. An increase in those species which constitute the food supply of another will diminish the number of deaths though it may not change the number of births. Hence, the population of the latter species, if it was in equilibrium before, is likely to increase. As the population of any species increases, it is likely to run into the famous Malthusian principle of an increasingly unfavorable environment. As a population increases, the number of deaths per unit time will increase until it equals the number of births, at which time the population is in equilibrium. If we suppose that the birth rates and death rates of each population can be written as functions of the sizes of all other populations in the environment, we get a set of n equations and n unknowns which may or may not have a positive solution for all populations. If it does, then we have an ecological equilibrium; if it does not, then the most vulnerable species will disappear one after another until an equilibrium is possible. This is the essence of the process of selection. The concept of a population as a set of objects with births into it and deaths out of it is highly general and applies not only to biological species but also to social species such as artifacts, organizations, and even to ideas and to the structure of knowledge. Even knowledge dies with the mind that contains it and has to be born in each generation into new minds through the process of teaching and learning. The equation of ecological equilibrium may be written as follows:

Birth Equation
$$b_i = F_b (X_1, X_2 - X_n) \qquad (1)$$
Death Equation
$$d_i = F_d (X_1, X_2 - X_n) \qquad (2)$$
Equilibrium Condition
$$b_i = d_i \qquad (3)$$

Suppose we have n species in an interacting system, where X_i is the population of the i_{th} species at a given time, then suppose that b_i is the number of births and d_i the number of deaths of the i_{th} species in a given period. For the species i, we can then postulate three equations which must be fulfilled in equilibrium; a birth equation (1), a death equation (2), and an equilibrium condition (3); births = deaths. With three similar equations for each species, this gives us $3n$ equations. We will also have $3n$ unknowns, the n populations, the n births, and the n deaths. For an ecological equilibrium, all these variables must be positive. If, for instance, when these equations are solved, X_i turns out to be negative, this population will disappear. A mutation consists of a new species, $n + 1$, which will change all the equations. It will survive if the new equations produce a solution in which X_{n+1} is positive. Survival value, then, is simply the ability to fit into an equilibrium ecosystem in such a way that births and deaths are equal with a positive population.

Human history, taken as a whole, is clearly more of an evolutionary process than it is either teleological or mechanical for it has no blueprint that we can perceive and cannot be described by differential equations. Like all evolutionary processes, its dynamic course must have some strong random elements in it. New mutations come into the world with some probability of survival. Even if a mutation only has a five percent probability of survival, it may survive, whereupon the whole future course of the process will be changed. Prediction, therefore, is severely limited in evolutionary processes. That is, simply knowing the previous history of the process does not permit us to project this history far into the future, unless the evolutionary process becomes teleological. This it increasingly tends to do after the evolutionary process itself has produced intelligence, for intelligent beings inevitably produce teleological processes. This, in fact, is a good operational definition of intelligence itself.

Up to the present, human history has been much more evolutionary than it has been teleological. Mutations occur in the form of new ideas, new inventions, prophets of new religions, organizers of new states, and conquerors of new empires. The process is a mixture of random and nonrandom elements, especially where we are concerned with impacts of charismatic personalities on history. If Jesus, Mohammed, Luther, or Hitler had died in infancy, the history of their own and of subsequent time would have been very different. There is some justification for thinking that the longer the period taken into consideration, the less important these random elements become. In teleological processes we can be reasonably sure of this. A strike, an accident, or a failure of supply of materials may delay the completion of a house, but are unlikely to alter the end product. Similarly some kind of deprivation may delay the growth of an animal, but if it is not fatal the animal will usually complete its course of growth. This course of growth of a teleological system has been called by biologists a *creode*. This is an equilibrium path of development implied in the original "blueprint." A temporarily adverse environment may produce divergences from the path, but such a divergence tends to create equilibrating forces that will bring process back to equilibrium path again.

In the case of the evolutionary process, we cannot be sure that there is any creode, or conversely, we can be confident that there are a large number of possible creodes or lines of evolutionary development. It may be that there are certain crossroads or watersheds in history where a slight random variation at a crucial time may carry the process in one of two different directions, just as a chance gust of wind on a raindrop falling on a watershed may determine whether it will flow into one ocean or another. Nevertheless, as we look at human history, and as we look at the wider spectacle of the whole evolutionary process, it does seem to have a direction or vector toward certain kinds of organization and complexity. We do perceive an evolutionary ladder ranging from inanimate matter, to the amoeba, to higher forms of life, culminating on earth in man. If an amoeba could argue with us, it might contend that this was an illusion of perspective arising from our regarding the universe through human eyes. Still, it is significant that an amoeba does not argue with us, and, hence, if progress is an illusion, it is one that is very difficult to shake. Similarly as we move from the paleolithic, to the neolithic, to civilization and into what I have elsewhere described as the post-civilized era,[1] it is hard not to perceive a direction that is not merely evolution but progress. In some areas of life the progress may be doubtful, and there are certainly ups and downs. But we can say that there are some important social quantities which exhibit cumulative change in a single direction.

This suggests that cutting across the classification into four types of processes which we have outlined above there is another classification which includes (1) equilibrium processes,

[1] K. E. Boulding, *The Meaning of the Twentieth Century*, Harper & Row, New York, 1965.

(2) cyclical processes, and (3) cumulative processes. An *equilibrium process* is one in which a disturbance from the equilibrium position results in a dynamic process to bring the system back once again to equilibrium. The equilibrium of the price system of the economists and the ecological equilibrium of the biologist are cases in point. Remove ten percent of a specific type of fish from a pond, and in two or three years the population distribution has returned to what it was before we disturbed it. Cut off the tail of a flat worm, and it will grow another. Destroy a city, and in a few years it is as populous as ever, even with many of the old buildings rebuilt. The equilibrium process is obviously real, both in biological and social systems.

A *cyclical process* is one in which a certain pattern is repeated over and over again. Some mechanical systems, such as the solar system or a clock, exhibit regular cycles—a day or a year for instance. Biological and social systems, likewise, often exhibit cycles which may be based on mechanical cycles such as the seasons or which may be transmitted into teleological systems such as the cycle in human activity of the day, the quarter, or the year. A university calendar is a good example of a cyclical teleological system. There may also be long cycles of prosperity and decline such as those supposed to have taken place about every eight hundred years in China. Evidences for these, however, are dubious. Many interpretations of history have assumed that history is essentially a cyclical process in which any apparent progress is merely an upswing in the cycle.

A *cumulative process* is one which never returns in any regular way to a previous position but which has a certain consistency in its pattern of change. Thus, most teleological processes are cumulative, at least if we exclude the very long run. The evolutionary process likewise is clearly cumulative, for there is no way back to any ecological equilibrium once it has been disturbed beyond a certain point. It must be admitted that many processes which look cumulative from the short run turn out to be circular in a long run. Still there seems to be a residue of genuinely cumulative processes which cannot be reduced to any circular form. Indeed, in evolution, we do occasionally perceive something like a cyclical process in reversion to a previous type after an extreme mutation. Nevertheless, these are strictly short term movements, and the long run movement in evolution is cumulative and irreversible.

Random processes are neither cumulative nor cyclical in essence, though over finite periods they may give an impression of being either. Even a random walker occasionally returns home, which may look like a cycle, and the longer the time we take the more cases we are going to find of his being a long way from home, which may look like a cumulative process. The human mind, furthermore, has a profound tendency towards superstition, that is, the imposition of a spurious order on its observations of random processes. Our "rage for order" makes us remarkably unwilling to admit that our information systems are inadequate to permit the perception of regularities and the consequent ability to predict, even where the regularities do not exist. We constantly need to be on our guard, therefore, against the tendency to read too much order into history, for if we do we are almost certain to be disappointed by our predictions of the future.

One aspect of this inclination to read into history more order than is there is a strong tendency to look for simple unitary explanations of all historical events in terms of some particular historical process. Economic interpretations of history attempt to interpret all phenomena in terms of certain economic events and processes. Religious interpretations seek to interpret history largely in terms of religious systems and institutions. There are political interpretations, military interpretations, and even climatic interpretations, all of which lay stress on a single process or system. It is clear that all these various systems are interrelated. It is clear, also, that some of them are more important than others. Nevertheless, all attempts to derive an interpretation of history from a single primary aspect of social life are doomed to failure.

In the biological world we have *ecosystems* such as lakes, swamps, forests, rivers, oceans, and different parts or regions of each, where there is very lively interaction of population within the system but not very much interaction between different systems. Similarly, in social life we find subsystems which have an intense interaction within themselves, a life and dynamic of their own, but where the interaction between different subsystems is tenuous even though, at times, important. It is possible, for instance, to have a society in which the economic system, the political system, the religious system, the military system, and so on actually pull in different directions for quite long periods of time. Some movements in the religious system have been favorable to economic development, and some religious movements have been adverse to economic development. Some movements in the religious system have been carried by the dynamics of the religious system itself, even to the detriment of political or economic welfare. We similarly find movements in political and military systems which have been highly adverse to economic development yet which have been carried by their own dynamics, sometimes to the very destruction of a society. Economic systems, likewise, have their own dynamics and can profoundly affect the political, religious, and social systems in which they are embedded. It is a dangerous oversimplification, therefore, to regard history as consisting of a determined mechanical process in a particular system from which all the other systems depend as appendages. All the various systems interact constantly, and one may be predominant at one time and not at another.

The sheer methodological problem of separating out not only the random from the nonrandom processes in history but also the interactions of various subsystems is difficult, and there are no simple formulas for solving this problem. Up to this point, the interpretation of history requires a certain poetic insight as well as the manipulation of statistical series. Sometimes a religion spreads because it has occupied a certain niche in a system of political discontent. Sometimes a political system, such as an empire, may spread because an otherwise unrelated religious change has given a society a dynamic morale and a sense of purpose. Economic change sometimes happens in a purely evolutionary way through the development of new processes and new commodities and their competition with the old in the market. Sometimes economic change develops in a teleological way through a deliberate investment plan.

The interpreter of history is in a dangerous occupation. Can he, at the same time, be sensitive to the movements of all social systems, avoid trying to confine history to any particular strait-jacket, beware of giving random events more importance than they deserve, be sensitive to the unnerving complexity both of man and of society, and still avoid the temptation to despair? The interpretation of his own history is for man an intellectual task of the highest practical importance, for only by understanding what is nonrandom in history can man hope to move from the slavery of evolution to the freedom of teleology. It is only as we learn the real processes of society that we can mold the future towards our present ideals. This is a task which requires a strange mixture of humility and boldness—humility to acknowledge that we may be wrong, for without this we cannot learn, and boldness to trust in our present understanding, for without this we cannot act.

CHAPTER 2
ORGANIZERS OF SOCIAL EVOLUTION

We can look at human history primarily as an extension of the evolutionary process from the biological into the social system. This is not a new idea. It goes back at least to Herbert Spencer. Nor does it imply that evolutionary processes are the only processes in human or any other history. Nevertheless, insofar as evolution is an essential part of machinery of change, we need to see how far we can go with this model before we have to turn to others. The evolutionary model, as we saw in the last chapter, consists essentially in a process of the creation, or appearance, of new species, and the constant selection of species through the process of moving towards a succession of ecological equilibrium states.

Biological evolution

In the biological world we can distinguish between two kinds of processes, those which involve the genotype and those which involve the phenotype. There is an old conundrum, "which came first, the hen or the egg?". The egg represents the genotype, the hen the phenotype. In the process of biological evolution, the most significant mutations occur in the genotype, that is, in the genetic material or genes, while the selective process operates mainly through the phenotype, that is, the living creature which the egg produces. Genes contain information which by a teleological process produce the phenotype of plant, animal, or human being. The phenotype in turn through its powers of procreation, whether sexual or asexual, transmit the genetical material into a new "egg," which again has the power of becoming another element in a population of phenotypes. Significant mutations can only occur in the genes, because these are the carriers of the information structure which perpetuates the population of phenotypes. Selection, on the other hand, can only occur among the phenotypes because the power of genes to survive depends only on the power of survival of the phenotype which it creates. We can see, incidentally, that much of the argument about the inheritance of acquired characteristics is an argument about whether events in the life of the phenotype can affect the genetic material which it carries. The answer seems to be that while some events such as being exposed to radiation may affect the genetic material, most of the ordinary events in the life of the phenotype do not. This does not preclude the possibility that an intelligent phenotype, such as man, may learn how to affect directly his own genetic material.

Once man appears on the earth, evolutionary change accelerates, almost as if the process steps into a higher gear, primarily because of the extraordinary learning capacity of the human nervous system and the power of man to develop language. Because of this, man is able to develop a new kind of species, social species, which includes his artifacts, his organizations, and his institutions. Social species are foreshadowed in the anthill, the beehive, and the wolf pack, though the single ant and bee are better regarded as elements in the larger biological complex of the nest or the hive, rather than as participants in true social systems. Automobiles, banks, churches, universities, states, and money are social species developed through the machinery of an evolutionary process within the human population. The genetics and the survival equations of the automobile are very different from that, say, of the horse. A new automobile is not produced in the womb of another automobile but in the womb of an automobile factory, and is produced by the direct organization of human ideas and knowledge into action. These differences, however, should not blind us to the fact that social species are true species, produced by a combination of genetic and teleological systems. The process by which social species succeed each other through time is parallel in many ways to the whole process of biological evolution.

Even the division between the genes and the phenotype carries over into social evolution, even though the genetic system itself and the process by which the genetic system gives rise to the phenotype is much more elaborate in social systems than it is even in biological systems. In social systems the gene is the image or the idea in the mind of man, ideas such as the plans recorded in the blueprint that create a building or an automobile, the idea or the image of the future that creates a new enterprise, the proposal of marriage that creates a new family, the image of a new kind of life in the teaching that creates a new religion. The parallel with the gene is exact. The essential structure of both consists in information, information which in a favorable environment is capable of creating a teleological process to produce the appropriate phenotype. The enormous increase in the rate of social evolution which took place after the appearance of man is due to the enormous power of the human nervous system and of language to code and transmit information. A group of monkeys have a primitive social structure and transmit this structure through a limited language consisting perhaps of a few dozen different visual and oral cues. The communication systems of animals, however, can only carry small loads of information. With the advent of human language, the information carried by the human information system increased perhaps by several orders of magnitude. This is why the appearance of man represents such an extraordinary acceleration of the evolutionary process.

Man's artifacts are the most visible and obvious social species, but we should not be deluded by their visibility or even by their durability into overestimating their importance. One of the dilemmas posed by the study of history is that the durability of artifacts, as opposed to the organizations which have produced them, introduces a bias into our information system. The *record* of the biological past consists mainly of genetic artifacts such as the bones and the shells of living creatures, which provided mere frameworks and housing for the living organisms that clothed or inhabited them. Similarly, the pottery, the houses, and even the writing of the human beings, which are the main records of the human past, are merely the skeletons and the shells of the social organizations which created them. There is a story of two cannibals watching an airplane fly overhead; one says to another, "It's very much like lobster. It's hard to get into, but very good once you get inside." The automobiles, airplanes, factories, houses, public buildings, and so on which surround us indeed bear much the same relation to the life which inhabits them as lobster shell does to the lobster. If indeed a being from outer space were observing this planet, he might well report that the process of evolution had produced a species of large four-wheeled bugs with soft detachable brains.

Human social organization

It is the social organization or organism which is, then, the prime species with which social evolution is concerned, and we need to examine how these come into being, grow, and develop. Human social organization presumably began when Adam met Eve. A social organization is present even when two men carry a single load, for even this simple act involves some kind of differentiation of roles, and a communication system between the occupants of these roles. A *social organization* is defined as role structure with a communication network uniting the occupants of the roles. The idea of the role is crucial to the understanding of organization; it can be thought of as a pattern of inputs and outputs which constitute the relevant behavior of the role occupant. Artifacts also occupy roles, and social organizations usually consist of persons and artifacts, such as machines or buildings, bound together by a network of inputs and outputs of energy, information, or objects. A person may be thought of as a number of different roles tied together by the fact that they all are performed by the same biological entity. The more developed the society, the more roles are likely to be combined in a single person, and some of the difficulties of a developed society arise from this, for the conflict of roles may produce disintegration of the human personality.

The next question is what processes in human relationships are capable of creating organization, that is, different roles united by an information system? Many such processes can be identified. They may conveniently be classified under three major heads which I call the threat system, the exchange system, and the integrative system. This corresponds

fairly closely to Sorokin's classification of human relationships into the compulsory, the contractual, and the fam-
ilistic.[2]

The threat system

A *threat system* begins when one person says to another,
"You do something nice to me or I'll do something nasty to
you." The subsequent course of the system depends on the
response of the threatened party. First, he may submit, in
which case what might be called an exploitative role structure is set up—B will be doing things for A and A will not
be doing much for B except threatening and abstaining from
carrying out the threat. Slavery is a good example of this
system.

A second response to threat is *defiance*. If carrying out a
threat is costly to the threatener, defiance may very well succeed, for the threat will not be carried out and the system
will return to something like the prethreat state. A third
possible response is *avoidance;* B will simply run away. His-
torically this is also of great importance and is probably the
major source of human migrations. It also gets institution-
alized in developed societies in the institutions of the market.
If a worker can quit the employer who threatens him, if a
wife can divorce her husband if he threatens her, if the citi-
zen can leave the country that threatens him, the power of
the threat system is clearly much diminished.

The fourth possible reaction to threat is *counter-threat.*
That is, B says to A, "If you do something nasty to me I'll
do something nasty to you." This is what is known today as
deterrence, and this also, at certain times and places, has
limited the power of the threat system. It is, however, an
inherently unstable system, if only because of a decline in

[2] Pitirim A. Sorokin, *Basic Trends,* World Union Goodwill, Dec. 1963,
p. 31.

the credibility of both threat and counter-threat as time goes along. The ability of a threat system to organize society depends on two elements, capability and credibility. The capability of the threatener in carrying out of threats depends on the perceived costs to him of carrying out the threat, discounted by the probability of having to carry it out. The credibility of a threat in the mind of the threatened party is what affects his behavior. The credibility of a threat that is never carried out continually depreciates and eventually is likely to reach the point where the counter-threat system passes over into defiance, at which point either the threat has to be carried out or the threat system collapses altogether.

The exchange system

The second relationship which is capable of producing social organization is *exchange*. Exchange begins by A saying to B, "If you do something nice to me I'll do something nice to you." If B then accepts the invitation, the exchange is consummated. The exchange system is both more stable, more beneficial, and has a much greater horizon of development than the threat system. It is, for instance, what the game theorists call a "positive sum game," that is, a series of events in which all parties can be better off, whereas the threat system is more likely to be a negative sum game in that the threatener gains less than what the threatened party loses, though this is not universally the case. Exchange, as Adam Smith pointed out so well, tends to produce a division of labor which increases productivity and so adds to the positive sum aspects of the ultimate consequences. It is true that there are conflicts in exchange, especially over the ratio of exchange, for even though both parties are better off, the distribution of the total gain will go more to the seller if the price is high and to the buyer if the price is low. This fact has blinded many people to the essentially positive sum aspect of exchange, assuming of course that it is uncoerced and not admixed with threat systems and that there are some defences against deceit and ignorance.

The exchange system is peculiar in that many of its organizing powers lie at an unconscious level. The threat system is apt to be high in conscious awareness. When a robber says, "Your money or your life" or the state says, "Pay your taxes or we put you in jail" this is at a level of communication high up in the scale of conscious awareness. Exchange, by contrast, operates almost at the unconscious level. The shopkeeper does not shout to us, "Give me your money or I'll give you a loaf of bread" and for the most part sits quietly behind the counter waiting for us to come. Hence, the communication that is implied in the offer of exchange belongs to the level of things which are implicit and understood rather than explicit and highly conscious. For this very reason the power of exchange as a organizer is apt to be underestimated.

The integrative system

The third system, which I call the *integrative system,* is perhaps too complex and diverse to be classified under a single heading. Nevertheless, it is convenient to have a single heading under which we can put status relations, love and affection as well as hatred and mistrust, the learning process, the process by which culture is transmitted from one generation to another, the processes by which persons and institutions acquire dignity, respect, legitimacy, and so on. The integrative relationship is typified by A saying to B, "You do something for me because of what I am and what you are; because I am your father, or a king, a priest, a teacher, lover, child, or student, and so on." The integrative system is the least understood and least studied of the three. In the long run it may turn out to have the widest horizon of development and to be the most important. The integrative system is of great importance in the creation of churches, schools, families, and even states, for it is only as the threat system begins to absorb an integrative element and naked coercion is replaced by law and legitimacy that political institutions begin to acquire stability and the power of growth.

All social organizations without exception are built up by processes which can be classified into these three general types, though the proportions of threat, exchange, and integration which go into them differ profoundly. This is as true of formal organizations as it is for informal, casual, and impermanent relationships and associations. At one corner of the scale we have what is almost a pure threat system such as the highwayman. Between the armed robber and his victims there is little in the way either of exchange or integration. Even here, however, there is a background in the integrative system. For the moment the robber produces a gun he will assume a *status,* and both his behavior and the behavior of the victim depend in part on their images of the status system derived from their previous life experience. The system is not true exchange. Nevertheless, the threat, in a sense, has set off an exchange situation in which the life of the victim is now the property of the robber so that the robber in his threat says, "You give me your money and I'll give you your life."

At another corner of the continuum we have the operations which take place in organized commercial markets which seems to be almost pure exchange. Nevertheless, these take place in a setting of status, trust, and respect without which the exchanges would be impossible. They also take place in the setting of law and sanctions against nonperformance of contract which essentially belong to the threat system, which likewise makes these exchanges possible.

The family is an institution in which the integrative system is very strong and in which love, affection, status, and respect are strong motivators. Nevertheless, exchanges always are present, and if one member of the family feels that he is giving a great deal and not getting very much out, the contract on which the family implicity rests may break down. Similarly, the role structures and behavior in a family are frequently ordered by means of threat—the threat of punishment in ordering the relations of parents and children, the threat of separation or divorce in organizing the relationship of the parents themselves. Even in the most loving and idealistic Utopian community, there are limits on the terms of trade of the individual which will persuade him to stay within it, and likewise there is also the threat of expulsion against the nonconforming member.

By contrast with these extreme cases, there are some institutions which seem to combine all three systems in roughly equal proportions. I once conducted a little experiment by asking a group of students to rank, for a number of different social institutions, which of the three organizing systems, threat, exchange, or integration, was the most important, which was second in importance, and which was third. For some types of organization, there was substantial agreement. When it came to organizations such as the national state, there was no agreement at all, some seeing it as primarily a threat system, some as an exchange system, some as an integrative system. The conclusion which I drew from this is that in the case of those institutions where there was no agreement, the three systems were all present in about an equal degree and that hence there would be wide differences of estimates as to which was the most important.

We can express these relationships diagramatically by drawing an equilateral triangle, as in Figure 1a–b, where the point A stands for 100 percent integrative relationship, point B 100 percent threats, and point C 100 percent exchange. Any point within the triangle, such as K, then represents a division of the proportions between the three elements. Thus, if we draw KD parallel to AC, KE parallel to

AB, and *KF* parallel to *BC, K* represents a situation with a proportion *KD* of integrative relationship, *KE* of threats, and *KF* of exchange. It is easy to prove geometrically that no matter where the point *K* in the figure, the sum *KD* + *KE* + *KF* is equal to *AB* or 100 percent. I have sketched into the figure some guesses at the proportion of the three elements represented in various social institutions. The reader may put in his own guesses.

The learning process

Each of these three processes can be viewed as an aspect of a larger and more fundamental process which underlies all human history and indeed, broadly interpreted, the whole evolutionary process. This is the *learning process.* Human beings differ from all other creatures in the extent to which the information content of the phenotype or adult person is derived from experience, that is, from the inputs and outputs of the person himself, rather than from the genes or genetic materials. The ant knows how to be an ant because its genes have built this knowledge into its nervous system in much the same way that a blueprint can build behavior into the machine which is constructed from it. The kitten has to learn something of how to be a cat from his mother. Man as to learn almost everything about how to be a man from his experience. He comes into a world with huge potential and very little else; it is the input from other humans which turn us into human beings. Everything that happens to us teaches us something whether this was intended or not, that is, changes our image of the world around us. A credible threat may teach a man to be submissive, especially when its credibility is enlivened by the observation of the threat being carried out on others. Exchange likewise is a powerful teacher. If we produce something and find that there is a market for it and that we can get things we prefer in the exchange, this has already taught us to go on producing it.

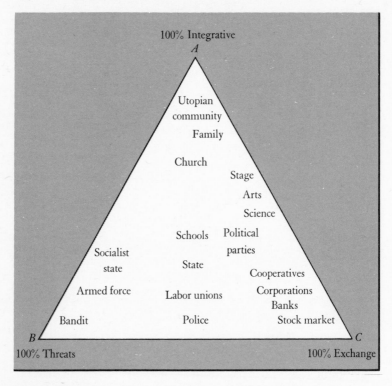

Figure 1-a. The social triangle (without connectives)

On the other hand, if we produce something and there is no market for it, we soon learn not to produce it. In the subtle exchanges of personal relationships we learn to grow up into adulthood, how to manage our conflicts, how to rationalize our defeats, and how to produce an output which in turn results in input from others. Learning in the integrative system is more complex partly because of the complexity of the system itself and partly because it is deeply involved in the learning of values.

The learning of values
The learning of values is perhaps that part of the learning process which is least understood, even though it is of an

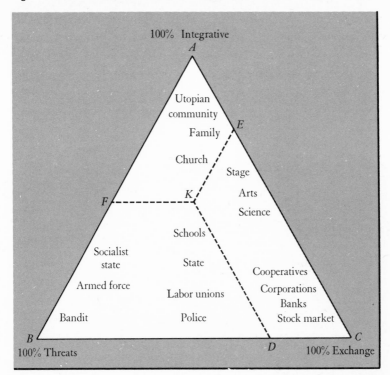

Figure 1-b. *The social triangle (with connectives)*

enormous importance in explaining not only the dynamic processes which make the individual what he is but also the larger processes of development of society. Like all animals, man enters the world with a primitive value system which seems to be genetically determined, that is, built into the nervous system by the genes. Straight from the womb we like milk, we dislike loud noises, and we dislike falling. The values associated with sex certainly have a genetic component, but even this is overlaid with values derived from culture and experiences. Moral values, esthetic values, and even most preferences for commodities are strictly learned. Food that one culture regards as delicious, another culture rejects as nauseous. Even pain, which seems to be a genetically produced negative value, may acquire a positive value in some cultures. There seems also to be a genetic and physiological basis for pleasure. In the rat we can locate and stimulate directly the pleasure center, and it is certainly not impossible we might do this for man. But here again some cultures value pleasure in this sense more highly than others, and some even value it negatively.

Learning, at least at its lower levels, is inextricably involved with rewards and punishments, that is, with high values and low values. What is not clear is how we learn what *are* rewards and what *are* punishments. Beyond the simple genetic level, the values on which most of human behavior is based have to be learned. Unquestionably, the child learns many of his values from his parents by association of cultural values with the genetic because the genetic values are so deeply associated with parental care. A child acquires the cultural values of its parents or may react against them if its genetic values are not adequately satisfied. There is a great deal of validity in the psychoanalytical view that many basic values, both conscious and unconscious, are determined in the first months of life. On the other hand, there are also value-forming influences which operate throughout life, especially in formal education and in adolescence. The general disposition toward certain values is unquestionably formed in infancy, but the particular conscious form which this disposition will take is more likely to be determined in later life. In any case, the individual from the moment of birth—and even before—is subjected to an enormous input of information, partly from his senses, partly from his internal information generators in the imagination, which itself is a powerful source of human learning, and, partly, once he has learned language, from the torrent of linguistic input which flows over and through him in most of his waking moments. From this torrent of information, the individual somehow selects the droplets from which he distills his image of the world.

When we look upon the process of learning in society as a process by which the stock of knowledge contained in the human population changes through time, we are immediately struck by the importance of the sheer biological fact of death. For all practical purposes we can say that nobody now living was alive a hundred years ago. The problem of passing on the stock of knowledge of a society from one generation to the next is perpetually urgent and is a dominant aspect of the dynamic processes of society. It is not merely poetic insight that proclaims "the child is the father of the man." The processes of transmitting the knowledge stock within the family, in the peer group, through formal education, and through written words and other records is the real heart of the historical process.

In paleolithic society, where the numbers of human beings in effective contact was very small, where the length of life was short, and where there was no written record, it seems to have been impossible to maintain a long cumulative process of growth in the stock of knowledge. The knowledge in the minds of old men or even in the young men was often removed by death before it could be passed on to the children. There must have been innumerable heartbreaking setbacks in which knowledge accumulated over several generations would be wiped out in an epidemic or a raid from another tribe or band. Just how man got out of this trap is by no means clear, but the critical process was clearly the domestication of crops and live stock and the invention of agriculture, perhaps ten thousand years ago. This increased the expectation of life, permitted the accumulation of food stocks, and permitted settlement in permanent villages. With the invention of writing, the accumulation of knowledge was released from the limitation of the single human mind and the precariousness of human memory. History in the sense of an image of a succession of events through time extending far beyond the present memory comes into existence. This concept deeply modifies human values and behavior.

The rise of science marked a change in the processes of the accumulation of knowledge as significant as the invention of language itself. It introduced a process of rapid and orderly change in the image of the world as it was present in the minds of members of the scientific sub-culture. It did this by a process of constant testing of predictions and refinement of perception. The accumulation of knowledge is essentially a process by which man's image of the world is changed. There are three major processes at work here. The first, prediction, the second, fulfillment or disappointment of the prediction, and the third, image-change as a result. Folk knowledge, the ordinary knowledge of life, is often hard to test and the images which embody it are hard to change. If the predictions which are made from folk knowledge are disappointed, there is a tendency either to deny the messages which indicate the disappointment or there is a tendency to deny the inference which gave rise to the prediction. Consequently, the image itself is hard to change, especially where the predictions are vague and ambiguous and the messages from reality hard to compare with the predictions. Folk knowledge is often transmitted by rote and is untested. Nevertheless, it must contain substantial elements of truth or it will not survive, simply because the people who hold widely untrue images do not survive. This, however, is blind selection and may select many images which are untrue, as well as much knowledge that is true. Prescientific societies, for instance, have a good deal of knowledge about how to plant, cultivate and reap crops. Some of this knowledge obviously is true, otherwise these societies would not have survived. On the other hand, the true knowledge may be accompanied by a great deal of superstition which survives because there is no way of separating it from the true knowledge. Both true and false images survive because the mixture as a whole has adequate survival value.

The scientific method by contrast tests particular images

directly. Predictions are drawn not from the simple projection of experiences but from a map or model from which
predictions are derived by a process of logical or mathematical inference. Predictions are made in a form such that ful-
fillments or disappointments can be determined without
much doubt, especially with the aid of devices which increase the resolving power of observations, such as the telescope and microscope. In a scientific sub-culture, if a prediction is not fulfilled, it does not take the death of the scientist to prove the corresponding image false. The process
operates directly on the image itself, for when we can deny
neither the observation nor the inference, the only course left
is to modify our image of the world. Science, therefore, has
introduced an evolutionary (selective) process operating directly upon knowledge itself, in which the survival of an
image depends on its own power of prediction, not on the
survival of the culture which holds it in its heads. It is little
wonder that it has resulted in an enormous acceleration in
the rate of accumulating knowledge and a corresponding increase in man's power.

One of the most crucial questions of the present day is
whether the rise of the social sciences may not lead to an
increase in man's power over his own history and over the future of his own societies akin to the increase of his power
over the physical world. Problems of the social sciences are
much more difficult than those of physical sciences for many
reasons. Random elements are more important. The knowledge that we seek to obtain from a social system is not only
the same order of magnitude as the system itself but an
essential part of it. Hence, we cannot find out anything about
a social system without changing it, and our predictions are
always in the form of probabilistic statements. Under these
circumstances, the testing of predictions and therefore the
testing of models from which they are derived is always
in some doubt, especially where the cases are few as is the

case with concrete historical systems. Suppose, for instance, we predict an event with 90 percent probability. If we are disappointed, we may just have been unlucky, and if the prediction is fulfilled, it may have been for the wrong reasons. The regularities of social systems are by their very nature elusive.

Nevertheless, we have developed both theoretical models of a reasonably precise nature and also a great improvement in our observational powers through such devices as sample surveys, statistical processing, and social indices. These devices for social instrumentation are already beginning to exert an influence on human history and may be expected to exert an even greater influence in the future. They represent not so much a sharp break with the past, as a further development and acceleration of that process of knowledge accumulation which is the most important single key to history.

CHAPTER 3
DIALECTICAL PATTERNS
IN HISTORY

The term *dialectical* as a pattern of social process is most generally associated with the name of Hegel, though the idea itself, like most others, can be traced in one form or another back to Plato. It has become a kind of sacred word in the Marxist faith, and in the process of becoming sacred, it has come to mean so many different things that it has lost much of its content. When Engels, for instance, calls dialectics "the science of general laws of motion both of the external world and human thought" [3] the term has surely become so broad as to lose all its specific meaning. I propose, therefore, to use the term in a narrower, more Hegelian

[3] *Karl Marx and Friedrich Engels on Religion,* Foreign Languages Publishing House, Moscow, p. 249.

sense, to describe those processes in history which have the familiar three-fold succession in time: thesis—antithesis—synthesis. The implication here is that we start with some kind of system or thesis which has a contradiction implicit in its own development, a contradiction which eventually "negates" the system and brings about its opposite or antithesis. This second system in term, however, will also have a contradiction in its development, a contradiction which eventually produces a third system, the synthesis, by another process of negation. The negation being negated, the synthesis is much like the original thesis. The process, of course, does not stop there but continues into a fresh antithesis and a fresh synthesis and either goes on forever or reaches some kind of final equilibrium. The model represents an attempt to apply some principles of formal logic to the empirical processes of history in the real world. As with all such models, however, the critical question is not in its internal consistency so much as its correspondence with actual processes.

Cyclical process

In its simplest form the process is purely cyclical. The synthesis is a simple repetition of the thesis and the process repeats itself indefinitely. It is, however, not a simple cyclical process like the rotation of the earth and the sun which produces the cycle of the seasons. It is rather a double cycle involving two variables, one of which rises while the other falls. Thus, in Figure 2, where time is measured horizontally and other variables vertically, the solid line would represent a simple cycle such as the solar cycle, whereas the dialectical process of the cyclical type would be represented by the combination of the solid and the dotted lines. If we call our two variables S and D at time T_1, S is in the ascendent (S_1) and D is in its trough (D_1). The internal processes of the system, however, call upon S to decline and D to rise. At R_1, where the two lines intersect, there is a "revolution," when D first becomes dominant over S. So we pass from the thesis at time

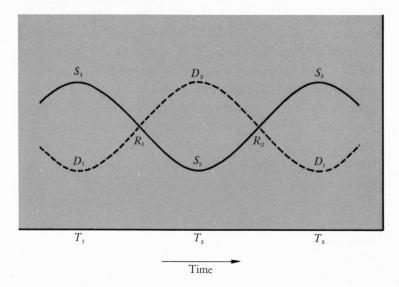

Figure 2. The dialectical process

(T_1) to the antithesis at time (T_2), where the relative position of the two variables are reversed. The process continues, however, with D declining and S advancing. There is another revolution at R_2, and eventually we have the synthesis at T_3 which simply repeats the position of T_1 from which point the system repeats itself indefinitely. This is what might be called the pure dialectical process. In this case what is meant by *contradiction* is simply instability. In the minds of most adherents of dialectical philosophy, however, the processes are essentially conflictual. We do not simply swing in opposite directions, like two pendulums out of phase. The process proceeds by the conflict between the two variables in which at each revolution point the dominant variable "loses" to the other, and the positions of dominance are reversed. In order for the antithesis to follow from the thesis, therefore, the D variable must "win" in its struggle against the S variable. Similarly, the passage from the antithesis to the synthesis represents a subsequent reversal of this process in which S "wins" over D at the point R_2.

For Hegel himself, and most subsequent dialecticians, the process has not been regarded as purely cyclical but as containing a cumulative element. It might be described as a spiral rather than a cycle, for the synthesis is not supposed merely to indicate a return to the position of the thesis but an advance to some superior position. It is seldom made clear where the cumulative aspect, or what might be described as the trend of the dialectical process, comes from. The simplest model would seem to be that the trend comes essentially from a *learning* process and that the experience of the conflict and succession of thesis and antithesis exercises a teaching function which prevents the system falling back into a condition identical with that of the thesis. The question whether the cumulative aspect of the dialectical process should be regarded as arising from nondialectical elements superimposed on the dialectical process which is regarded essentially as cyclical, or whether the cumulative process is supposed to arise as a result of the dialectical process itself is a matter of a considerable debate which we will touch upon in the next chapter. We must notice, however, that the dialectical process, as I have described it, is not a true model of a dynamic process. It is a description rather than an explanation. If a genuine model has to be constructed, certain extraneous assumptions must be introduced with regard to the nature of dynamic processes themselves. The analogy of logical contradiction is quite inadequate to explain any "mechanical" dynamic process. We must have something that looks like a difference or differential equation, relating in a unique way two or more successive states of the system.

Dialectical process in nature

Suppose, then, that we look at the world of nature to see whether there is anything that looks like a dialectical process that can be described in the above terms. At the level of simple mechanical processes, we have many cyclical processes, but practically nothing which looks like a dialectical process. The swing of a pendulum or the rotations of the planets are cyclical, not dialectical. By an act of poetic fancy, we can imagine that the orbit of a planet around the sun is the result of a "struggle" between two dialectical forces, centrifugal and centripetal. But this is just that—poetic fancy. It makes no contribution to the real understanding of the equations of the system. It is possible to construct a mechanical dialectical machine, which is illustrated in Figure 3. Suppose we have two vessels, *A* and *B,* mounted on a rather stiff axle, *C*. When water is poured into the upper vessel *A* until some point where the equilibrium of the system is up-

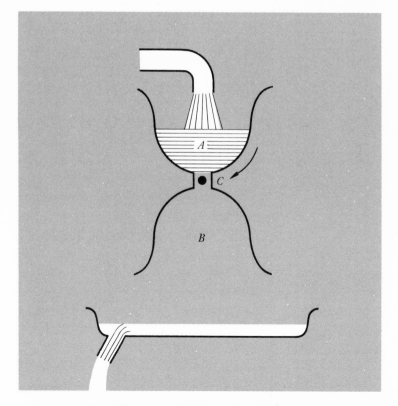

Figure 3. A dialectical machine

set, a revolution, more exactly a half-revolution, occurs. *A* pours its water down the drain and *B* becomes uppermost, symbolizing the passage from the thesis to the antithesis. Then, as the water accumulates in *B* another half-revolution occurs. *A* becomes uppermost, and the thesis is restored in the synthesis. The fact that it takes a contrivance as absurd as this to illustrate the dialectical process in mechanical systems is a testimony to the uselessness of the model at this level.

In biological systems, we do get something which looks like a dialectical process in the succession of the generations and especially the succession of phenotype and genotype. This again is typified by the hen–egg–hen succession. The hen as thesis produces the egg as the antithesis; the egg as antithesis produces the hen again as synthesis. In the succession of the generations we perceive something that looks even more like a dialectical process. Between fathers and sons, there is certainly a type of conflict in which the sons eventually "win" and become fathers in their turn, only to be defeated by their sons, and so the cycle goes on. At some point in the cycle, every man says of his son or of the younger generation, "he must increase but I must decrease." [*John, 3:20*] There may be a cumulative process in all this; the grandsons may be better and wiser than the grandparents, so that the synthesis is indeed not a mere recapitulation of the thesis. The important question for dialectical philosophy is whether the superiority of the grandchildren arises from the contemplation of the struggle between their grandparents and their parents or whether it arises from other causes.

In terms of biological evolution, however, the dialectical pattern contributes practically nothing to our understanding of the process. First, it is not any internal contradiction in the system which produces change. In ecological succession, for instance, it is the process of a random mutation in the genetic material which introduces, as it were, altogether new equations into the equation of ecological equilibrium. Second the process by which one ecological equilibrium is succeeded by another as a result of genetic mutation is such a complex mixture of competitive and cooperative elements that it cannot be described usefully in terms of a dialectical conflict. The new equilibrium does not represent an antithesis which "fights" with the old equilibrium of the thesis; it represents simply a new solution of a new set of equations. It is not even true that all populations are in competitive relationships with all others. There are complex symbiotic networks and, in a very real sense, the achievement of any ecological equilibrium is a "victory" for mutuality and unconscious cooperation. Even the predator is an important element in the biological survival of its prey: the wolf is necessary to the deer. There is a struggle for survival, but this cannot be described in terms of any simple pattern of conflict. Any attempt to force the description of biological evolution into a dialectical pattern, therefore, results in a gross distortion. That unfortunate phrase "the survival of the fittest," which gave rise to so many false analogies, is almost devoid of content, for, in this context, by "fittest" we mean merely fit to survive. Therefore, all the phrase means is the survival of the surviving, which does not tell us very much. As we seek to put content into the evolutionary pattern, it becomes apparent that the process of mutation and selection and the processes of ecological equilibrium and succession can only be described as dialectical by draining the term of all intellectual content.

Dialectical process in social systems

As we turn to social systems and to human history, we begin to find more examples that look like dialectical processes. While the succession hen–egg–hen is nondialectical in its essence, the succession grandfather–father–son may contain systematic elements which deserve the name of dialectic. Virtually all the dialectical elements in the social process, however, are contained in what I have called in the previous chapter the *threat system*. The dialectical element is relatively unimportant in exchange, and it is very rare in the integrative system.

As we search through history looking for patterns similar to that in Figure 2, we find them mainly in the records of wars and revolutions, both of which are examples of threat systems. We observe, for instance, the successions of states and empires. Sumeria, Babylon, Egypt, Greece, and Rome rise and fall and succeed each other largely through conflict. Similarly, factions or classes within a state may likewise rise and fall and succeed each other through the process of revolution or internal shift of power. In these histories there are frequently revolution points like R_1 and R_2 in Figure 2 at which a previously subordinate party becomes dominant and the previously dominant party becomes subordinate. A revolution point is seldom passed without violence, although relatively nonviolent revolutions, such as the "Glorious Revolution" of 1688 in England, have occurred, especially in more sophisticated and developed social systems. It is worthwhile, therefore, looking into the nature of threat systems, to see if, in fact, a dynamic model can be developed which corresponds to the dialectical description. We find not only that a model of a threat system which exhibits the dialectical pattern is fairly easy to construct but also that conflict systems, which are a more general category than threat systems, may likewise give rise to processes which have the dialectical description.

A threat system begins, as we saw in the preceding chapter, when A says to B, "You do something nice to me or I'll do something nasty to you." It is only possible to organize such systems, of course, if B is in the position to do something "nice" for A. This can only happen if B has some kind of surplus above and beyond what he needs for his own subsistence and survival. In a threat-submission system, A is able to take the surplus from B, and with this he is able to organize the threat which causes B to submit. A king, for instance, can feed his army, which he uses to threaten his slaves, with the surplus food the slaves produce. This, in itself, is a highly stable system without any inner contradiction, and no dialectical process can emerge out of it. The extraordinary stability of isolated civilizations, like that of Mohenjo-daro, and even of isolated neolithic villages, is a tribute to the stable and nondialectical characteristics of a simple threat-submission system. The dialectical process only arises if a threat-submission system passes over into threat-defiance or threat-counterthreat. This can happen because the capability of the threatener to carry out his threats and also the credibility of threats tends to diminish the farther away from the threatener one gets, either in space or in time. At some point, therefore, either in space or in time, the threat-submission system becomes unstable. The threatened party B defies the threat made by A when he gets far enough away from its point of origin, and if he is successful in this he is able to erect a threat system of his own. The system is illustrated in Figure 4. A is the original threatener, and suppose that we reduce his location to the single point on a line such as AB. The credibility of the threat we represent by the line $A'V$ and a similar line to the left of A. If A is unchallenged, he can presumably organize society to support him within the distance AV from his own base. There may be other threat systems beyond V, but these do not introduce any instability into the system. This would be like, for instance, relations between Sumeria and Mohenjo-daro.

In a system such as this there is a chance for an "upstart" to arise, perhaps from around the limit of A's credibility at V, perhaps even closer to A, say at B, where A's threat is so attenuated by distance that B has the chance first to defy

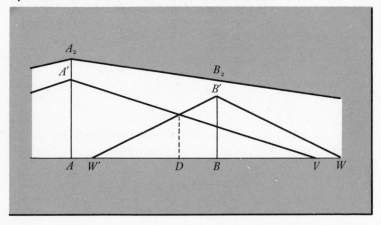

Figure 4.   Competition between two parties

the threat, secondly to erect a counterthreat system of his own as represented say by the line $W'B'W$. We now find a critical location D which we call the boundary of equal strength. B's threats are superior to A's at any point to the right of D. A's are superior to B's at any point to the left of D. Even a system of this kind is not necessarily dialectical. It may for a time be stable and result in co-existence, even peaceful co-existence. Under circumstances which are not at all improbable it becomes unstable, and one party tries to eliminate the other. Suppose, for instance, that A raises his threats to the line A_2B_2 where his threats are now superior to B's even at the point B. A is now in the position to eliminate B altogether as A's threats are superior to B's at any point of the field, and B will have to return to submission or extinction. On the other hand, it is possible that B, by raising its threat sufficiently, might do the same thing to A and force A to submission or extinction. Only in the latter case do we have anything that looks like a really dialectical process. The first case is that of unsuccessful rebellion or revolt, whereas dialectical process implies that revolt against the original threatener can be successful. The original possessor of the threat system, in this case *A,* has certain advantages, and most revolts are, in fact, unsuccessful.

Processes of a successful revolt

If we are really to have a dialectical process emerge out of our dynamics, therefore, we must ask what are the processes that can lead to a *successful* revolt. For this we have to appeal to the principle of the depreciation of credibility of threats with distance in time as well as in space. The credibility of threats is usually established at a certain point of time by the carrying out of some previous threat, whether explicit or merely implied, in a shape of a war or battle or the overthrow of a previous power. As time goes on the memory of events which led to the establishment of credibility of the threat becomes weaker. The original conqueror is perhaps succeeded by his sons and grandsons. Capability of carrying out threats is also likely to diminish. Indeed the credibility often persists long after the capability has declined, but eventually the process of erosion of credibility goes on and we reach a point at which the threat is challenged. If, at this point, *A*'s threat capability has seriously declined, the challenger may easily be successful, though he is likely still to be at a location some distance from the original center of power. This model suggests both the time pattern and the space pattern of the rise and fall of empires, and it is even possible to express this in rough quantitative terms, though random elements are still so important in such a system that the exact time and place of the rise of a new threat-power center cannot be predicted.

The model suggests a further important conclusion—that the diminution of what I call the "loss of power gradient," as measured for instance by the slopes of the line *A'V* or *B'W* in Figure 4, *increases* distance from the original center either in space or in time at which new centers of power can arise. This suggests that we have now come to a critical stage in human history, a stage at which the loss of power gradient both in space and in time has been so diminished by various technological changes that the dialectical process involved in this model is now close to an end. If the rise of a rival power center can only take place more than 12,500 miles from an old one, obviously on this earth the dialectical process in geographical space is over. This has nothing to do with who happens to be in power at the time, but it is simply concerned with the quantitative parameters of the system. The feeling which has been in the air for some time, that we are entering a new phase of human history, is well founded and can be deduced from the logic of the threat system model.

Revolution is a phenomenon somewhat similar to war, with social distance, replacing geographical distance as the essential variable of threat system. A particular faction, group, or class in society may organize a threat system and establish itself as the ruling group. Because it is the ruling group, however, it is cut off from effective two-way communications, with those outside it, and it establishes social distance between itself and the ruled. The ability of threats to organize the social system, that is, to produce submission, is closely related to the development of an integrative system, implying the legitimacy of the ruling group. It is much easier to obtain submission to an authority which is widely regarded as legitimate than to obtain submission to one that is regarded as illegitimate and only maintained in power by naked threats. Illegitimate threats rapidly produce defiance and counterthreat; threats which are regarded as legitimate do not. It is much harder, for instance, to organize effective resistance to the traffic cop than it was to organize resistance to the prohibition agent, because the first is largely regarded as legitimate, the second was not.

The dynamic processes by which legitimacy changes are

extremely complex and little understood. Why, for instance, did the Czar of Russia lose his legitimacy in the defeat of 1917, whereas the Emperor of Japan retained his, though in a somewhat modified form, after the equally disastrous defeat in 1945? Some legitimacy is established by conquest, that is, by the exercise of superior threat. This type of legitimacy frequently tends to erode with the passage of time, and eventually the threat system which is based on it can no longer be maintained. The development of democracy is the equivalent, in the sphere of social distance, to the reduction in the cost of transport and in the loss of power gradient in a geographical sphere. Revolution, like revolt, can only occur if the social distances between the ruler and the ruled are great. The forces of material technology, which have destroyed the dialectical process of war, likewise are at work in the social sphere destroying the dialectical process of revolution.

The theory of conflict processes can throw further light on the question of what determines whether a dialectical process of conflict is a cycle or spiral, and what determines whether the spiral goes up or down.

Suppose we have two parties in conflict, A and B. We can think of these as two different countries, two different classes, say, labor and management, two factions, or even two ideological positions. In a field, such as Figure 5, we measure A's welfare horizontally and B's welfare vertically, so that any point such as P_0 shows us a combination of welfare of the two parties, OB_0 measuring B's welfare and B_0P_0 A's welfare. From point such as P_0, four directions of movement can be identified. A move to the "northeast" toward P_b means that both parties are getting better off; the welfare of both parties is increasing. This I call a *benign* move. The opposite move to the southwest toward P_m, for instance, is a *malign* move in which the welfare of both parties diminishes. A move either to the northwest or to the southeast is a conflict

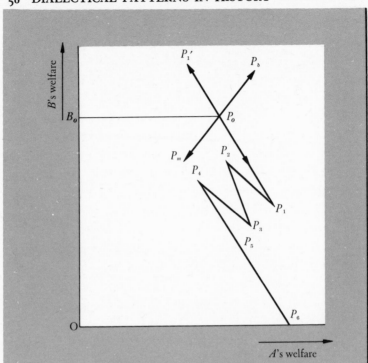

Figure 5. The dynamics of conflict

move. If we move to the northwest, for instance, toward P_1', B is getting better off while A is worse off. If we move to the southeast, say toward P_1, A is better off but B is worse off. In what might be called a *conflict dialectic,* we have a succession of conflict moves carrying us to positions such as $P_0, P_1, P_2, P_3, P_4, P_5$. A, shall we say, moves from P_0 to P_1. B retaliates to P_2. A retaliates, in turn, to P_3, B to P_4, A to P_5, and so on. A process of this kind has a strong dialectical pattern. If, for instance, in position P_0, A thinks he can do something which will carry the system to P_1 and he is short-sighted enough to think it will stay there, then we can regard the system at P_0 as containing a contradiction or at least an element of instability. Similarly, if B is capable of retaliating at P_1 to the position P_2, then the situation at P_1 likewise constitutes a contradiction. P_0 is a thesis, P_1 is an antithesis and P_2 is a synthesis and the new thesis from which we go on to P_3 and P_4. In this case, however, the succession of dialectical moves results in a malign movement of the whole system. As a result of a succession of conflict moves, both parties get worse off. A good example of this would be an arms race in international relations or a price war between two firms. We see this process also operating frequently in the quarrels of children. It occasionally operates also in industrial relations where the succession of strikes and lockouts can make both parties worse off.

It is possible, however, to reverse the process and for a conflict dialectic to result in a generally benign movement. We might, for instance, start at P_5 and move through P_4, P_3, P_2 and P_1 to P_0. In this case, even though in each conflict move one of the parties gets worse off, the overall result is that both parties get better off. The difference between a malign and a benign dialectic consists essentially in the quantitative parameters of the system. It is even possible to envisage a stationary or circular dialectic movement for instance from P_0 to P_1, back to P_0, back to P_1, and so on indefinitely, though a movement of this kind is hardly likely to be stable. The mathematical condition for a benign dialectic can be stated verbally by saying that each party should be able to regain in one move more than he lost in the move before. Thus, if we start at P_5 and B moves to P_4 with A losing, then if in a move to P_3, A's gain per unit of B's loss is greater than A's loss per unit of P_0's gain in a movement from P_5 to P_4, then P_3 will be likely to be a better position of *both* parties than at P_5, though this is not necessarily so. The actual mathematical conditions for an overall benign move have to be stated rather carefully and are a little difficult to translate to words.

In fact, malign dialectical processes seem to be much more

common than benign ones. An arms race is more frequent than a disarmament race, a rise in tension and hostility more common than a fall in tension and hostility, and so on. The crucial variable here might be called the *rate of conflict*. This is the ratio of the gain of the winning party to the loss of the losing party. In moving, say from P_0 to P_1, it is the slope of the line P_0P_1. The less the absolute value of the slope the less is B's loss per unit of A's gain. In moving from P_1 to P_2, it is the reciprocal of the slope of the line P_1P_2. If then c_a is the rate of conflict of A with B in one move, and c_b is the rate of conflict of B with A in the next move, then a necessary (though not sufficient condition) for a benign move is that c_ac_b should be less than one. If c_ac_b is greater than one, the moves will be malign; if it is equal to one, the moves will be neutral. The system will move back to its original position if the extent of each move is the same.

Rates of conflict are likely to be low when there are strong nondialectical elements in the situation, when, for instance, there is a good deal of benevolence, empathy, integration, and so on. By contrast, if there is a lot of class consciousness, race consciousness, and national consciousness leading to malevolence, that is, to positive satisfaction in the diminution of the welfare of others, the rate of conflict is likely to be high and the dialectical process is likely to be malign. We therefore encounter what may seem rather to be a startling conclusion that the dialectical philosophy, because it encourages conflict, hatred, class, race, national consciousness, and malevolence is likely to lead to a high rate of conflict and therefore to malign dialectical processes in which everybody gets worse off. The very success of the dialectical process, therefore, may depend on a wide spread acceptance of nondialectical philosophy and value systems. Dialectical philosopies such as Marxism, Fascism, nationalism, racism, and militarism are those which put a high value on conflicts as such and on "defeating the enemy." Nondialectical philosophies such as Christianity, Buddhism, psychoanalysis, social democracy, and social work, emphasize love, empathy, resolution of conflict, the redemption and integration rather than defeat of the enemy and therefore tend to develop low rates of conflict. History is full of examples of the enormously high cost of dialectical philosophies which have probably caused more human misery than any other error of which man's mind is capable.

The dialecticians may object that the process of mutual conflict which I have described in Figure 4 is not a truly dialectical process because it assumes that both parties remain in existence, whereas a true dialectical process is what game theorists call a *game of survival* in which one party is eliminated altogether. Suppose, for instance, that A can finally move to a point such as P_6 in Figure 5, where B is eliminated altogether and A's welfare is thereby increased to OP_6 and remains stable at this level, as B is no longer around to challenge him. This kind of thing has happened. *Cartago delenda erat* (Carthage was rubbed out). When the communists take over they eliminate the capitalists. Standard Oil eliminates its competitors. Then presumably everybody lives happily ever after. Games of survival, however, are terribly costly, even to the survivor. Furthermore, the one who starts them does not always have the best chance of winning them, and the stability which is obtained by eliminating a competitor seldom lasts long. Now, especially with the nuclear weapon, a game of survival might mean that nobody survived. Those who advocate such policies are literally playing with the future of man. This is the extreme position of the dialectical philosophy. In this extreme form it is a monster indeed.

CHAPTER 4
NONDIALECTICAL PATTERNS
IN HISTORY

The distinction between the dialectical and the nondialectical elements in history is not always a precise one. Important distinctions, however, seldom are precise. The categories shade into each other as colors do in the rainbow. Nevertheless, just as dialectical processes are characterized by circular, or spiral, sequences of events, by revolutions in which the position of two parties or factors is reversed, and by contradiction and conflict, so we may identify the nondialectical elements in history as those which are cumulative, involving steady growth or development, those in which the cyclical aspects are incidental to fundamental trends, and those which are nonconflictual or in which conflict is a minor and incidental element.

Biological evolution

The process of biological evolution on the whole seems to be nondialectical. Genetic mutations tend to be fairly small, and the evolutionary process proceeds by the continuous selection of small changes at the margin. This does not rule out the possibility of certain large mutations. Because of their rarity, however, these are virtually unobservable. We do indeed find ecological systems in which there may be "contradictions," but only in the sense that there are irreversible cumulative processes at work in them which will eventually change them. The life processes in a pond, for instance, may eventually turn it into a marsh, the marsh into a prairie, and the prairie into a forest. These successions, however, do not have a dialectical pattern. There is no "conflict" between the marsh and the pond, the pond does not suppress the marsh until the marsh gathers enough strength to effect a revolutionary overthrow. The transformations take place cumulatively and gradually, and though populations within the system are in conflict, the successive systems themselves are not.

Dialectical philosophers may argue that the role of catastrophes in the evolutionary process has a dialectical or at least a revolutionary element in it. Here again catastrophes, being by their very nature rare (otherwise there will be nothing left to study), are difficult to observe and their role is unclear. There is evidence, however, that catastrophes in the past, by destroying an equilibrium which had become too stable, have permitted new mutations to survive and hence have laid the foundation for a new evolutionary advance. It may well be, for instance, that the unknown catastrophe which destroyed the dinosaurs and led to the extinction of a very large number of species was an essential ingredient in the development of the mammals and the next age of evolutionary process. Catastrophe puts a premium on adaptability rather than adaptation. In times of catastrophe it is the meek, that is, the adaptable, who inherit the earth, whereas the strong who are well adapted to the environment which is passing away become extinct. In this connection it has been suggested that the Ice Ages played an important part in the development of man, simply because once again they gave a great survival value to adaptability.

However, we must not give these speculations about the role of catastrophe more scientific weight than they deserve. We do not here have a phenomenon which can be observed easily and repeated. While the argument that the catastrophe may have speeded up the evolutionary process has some probability, it may be doubted whether it plays a fundamental role. It seems likely, for instance, that, once the evolutionary process had produced the warm blooded animal, this type of life had substantial advantages over the reptile, even in the absence of catastrophe. Similarly, it is hard to believe that a fire-using animal, such as man, would not have great advantages even in the absence of the Ice Age. The catastrophes which have punctuated the evolutionary process are not in themselves dialectical, that is, they do not arise by necessity out of the contradictions of previous systems but are usually imposed from without. This is particularly true of climatic changes which do not in any way depend on the inner workings of a system of biological evolution, but are completely extraneous to it, even though they may have a great impact on it. One possible exception to this proposition is the climatic change which may result from the absorption of carbon dioxide from the air by plants and other living organisms and its present restoration to the atmosphere through the burning of fossil fuels. It has been suggested that an increase of carbon dioxide in the air will have a "greenhouse effect" and will upset the heat balance of the earth by letting more heat in through the atmosphere from the sun than it lets out at present temperatures. This would be expected to raise the temperature of the earth which would, of course, have profound consequences such as the melting of the ice caps and a change in the whole ecological structure of the biosphere. There may be long cycles of this kind in the evolutionary process which have something of a dialectical character to them in the sense that it is the contradictions within one phase that produce the next. There is no agreement among natural scientists, however, about the reality of these phenomena—thus the "greenhouse effect" may be literally overshadowed by increasing cloud cover and again they must be put in the category of interesting speculation.

In the case of social evolution, dialectical processes unquestionably do occur, but these are essentially temporary, short run, and minor in nature. The great changes are always nondialectical. They occur as a result of the cumulative impact of small changes and the selection of small social mutations. Furthermore, for the most part the great changes are nonconflictual. Who gets what is a minor and incidental aspect of a great process by which we all get more. The great changes in social system, furthermore, are nonrevolutionary in spite of the fact that we sometimes carelessly use the word revolution simply to mean a large change. It is highly misleading, to use the same word revolution both for the process of evolutionary or economic development as we do in the expression "industrial revolution" and for processes which mainly involve shifts in the locus of political power, such as the American, French, or Russian revolutions.

Because it is used for so many different phenomena, the use of the term revolution has become so confused that one is tempted to abandon it, though it is too well established for that. Perhaps we should distinguish between nondialectical revolutions and dialectical revolutions. The *nondialectical revolution* is a step function, that is, it represents discontinuity in the total evolutionary process because of some mutation which has a profound, long-term effect on the whole system. Thus, the evolution of life itself, of the vertebrates and especially of man, was a "revolutionary" step in this sense. These revolutions, however, are nondialectical in the sense that they do not emerge as a result of the conflict of two systems and the triumph of one system over another. The mutation which gives rise to revolutions of this kind indeed are frequently very small and quite imperceptible at the time. By contrast, *dialectical revolutions* involve the emergence out of one system of a rival system and the revolution takes place when the rival system overcomes the former one and supplants it. I argue, however, that dialectical revolutions are a small part of the total drama of the universe which is dominated by nondialectical revolutions and cumulative processes.

The growth of knowledge

The first great cumulative process which on the whole is nondialectical is the growth of knowledge. The growth of knowledge, as we have seen, can be described in terms of a mutation-selection process. As a result of certain inputs of information, whether from the outside or from his internal information generators, a man develops a change in his image of the world. At some point in the human story, perhaps at many points, somebody had the idea of planting an edible seed instead of eating it, the image being that plants grow from seeds. These images, then, undergo a selective process as they are tested in experience, and the true ones tend to pass more tests than the false ones. Sometimes, as we have seen, the test involves the survival of a whole culture in which false images as well as true ones survive, and conversely, true images as well as false ones fail to survive. As man gradually develops an apparatus for testing the images directly, a process which culminates in the subculture of science, his capacity for knowledge growth increases accordingly. This, however, is an evolutionary rather than a dialectical process.

That there are some dialectical elements in the growth of knowledge is suggested by the occasional use of the term *revolution* to describe some particularly dramatic restructuring of man's image of himself or his world. Thus, we talk about the "Copernican" revolution or the "Keynesian" revolution, and even though there are certain dangers in the loose use of this word, the analogy with political revolution is not wholly inept. In the replacement, for instance, of the Ptolemaic view of the universe by the Copernican, we can indeed trace something like a dialectical process. The old system has power, it is taught in the schools, and those who know it and teach it have a vested interest in preserving it. If, however, it is "wrong" in the sense that it has some internal contradictions or that it does not give a useful picture of reality, it will eventually be challenged by a new system. The new system at first is likely to command few adherents. Those who believe in it are likely to be young men who are ambitious but not powerful, and a conflict then ensues between the new view and the old, which ends in the triumph of the new view and a successful revolution. Here we seem to have a typical dialectical pattern where the old view is the established thesis, the new view is the antithesis, which is first of all subordinate to and in conflict with the old view, then finally triumphant over the established thesis. The new view, of course, may have some inner contradictions in it which will lead to the process being repeated over and over again.

On closer examination the dialectical description is much less satisfactory as a description of what actually goes on in the advance of knowledge. If, for instance, we examine the Copernican revolution more closely we find in the first place that the dissatisfaction with the Ptolemaic system arose mainly as a result of a slow cumulative improvement in the observation of the movement of the planets. We find, furthermore, that there were not simply two systems contending but many different suggestions and alternatives. Tycho Brahe, the famous Danish astronomer whose careful observations helped to undermine the Ptolemaic theory, himself, developed a version of the solar system, different from the Copernican or the Ptolemaic view. Furthermore, we find that Copernicus' own theory was as defective in many ways as the Ptolemaic system itself and completely failed to give adequate predictions. Copernicus, for instance, assumed that the planets moved around the sun in circles. It was not until the invention of the telescope enabled astronomers to make more refined observations and until Kepler and Newton provided an adequate mathematical basis for the view that the planets revolve around the sun that the solar-centric theory became really powerful and acceptable. Once it became powerful in prediction, it became universally accepted without further struggle. Thomas Kuhn's thesis in his *Structure of Scientific Revolutions* [4] is that science proceeds by two different kinds of processes—the ordinary process of research directed by existing theoretical frameworks and the "revolutionary" upheaval when an old framework is discarded and a new framework takes its place. This view does not, it seems to me, fundamentally contradict the thesis of this chapter. It is quite true that the cumulative processes of science are not simple and do not consist in simple aggregation. A scientific theory is a Gestalt, not a mere collection or dictionary. The formation of a new Gestalt is a process frequently accompanied by trauma, upheavals, turbulence, and conflict so that it is not wholly unreasonable to use the word "revolution" and to regard the formation of these new Gestalts as a dialectical process. I am arguing, however, that these dialectical processes which accompany scientific revolutions are costs, not revenues, and it is absurd to idealize

[4] Thomas Kuhn, *The Structure of Scientific Revolutions.* Chicago: University of Chicago Press, Phoenix Books, 1962.

them. They represent, as it were, the heat of crystallization in a process of essentially continuous change. The dialectical processes which they may introduce are a hindrance rather than a help to the growth of science. The comfort which dialectical philosophers seem to have drawn, therefore, from Kuhn's work seems to be based on a misunderstanding.

It is the reverse of knowledge, that is, ignorance, that makes for the dialectical pattern, and once knowledge is achieved the dialectical pattern immediately disappears. The dialectical part in the knowledge process is highly characteristic of ideology and speculation, but it is not characteristic of the growth of secure knowledge. An *ideology* may be defined as a particular view or image of the universe which is associated with particular centers of political or economic power. It is the association with power as embodied in a threat system that contributes to the dialectical pattern as we saw in the previous chapter. The dialectical pattern in ideology is essentially a property of the threat system because political power requires something more than the naked threat if it is to be effective. Otherwise, it becomes too costly to maintain. A center of political power nearly always attempts to become the center of an integrative system as well as a threat system, and the acceptance and propagation of an ideology by a center of political power may be interpreted, therefore, as an attempt to shift political power from the basis of pure threat to a basis of status, respect, and willing acceptance. The propagation of an ideology often enables the center of political power to develop an integrative system in which those who are subject to it come to accept it willingly. These ideological systems, however, suffer the same disability as threat systems in general. New centers of power may arise at a distance from the old, and these new centers will frequently seize upon a new ideology to differentiate themselves from the old centers and to build up an integrative system around them.

Thus, the dialectical struggles, let us say, between Christianity and Islam, between Catholicism and Protestantism, between Capitalism and Communism, are not essentially part of the knowledge process but are essentially part of the threat system. The growth of knowledge is not advanced by the dialectical process at all; it is hindered by it. Dialectical struggles prevent the testing of knowledge by direct or scientific methods, and they represent a backward step towards the testing of images by the success of whole cultures, not by the testing of knowledge itself. The dialectical process results in severe impairments of the knowledge-building process on both sides of a conflict, for when questions are posed in dialectical terms, that is, in terms of the conflict between two cultures or two power centers, each center gradually loses the ability to learn from the other. The value system of each, then, begins to operate as a filter to distort the process of information input, to filter out information which is contradictory to the particular ideology held, and, hence, to prevent learning. Beyond a certain point, conflict processes are not conducive to learning. They tend rather to the reinforcement of old images, no matter what they are and no matter how valid they are. The kind of testing of images that goes on in conflict is entirely different from the kind of testing that goes on in the scientific process.

Even within the subculture of science, of course, dialectical processes are not unknown. Scientists develop pet theories which they defend because they are involved with their personal prestige. Scientists are not devoid of human failings, and the image of the scientist as pursuing truth at all costs, even at the cost of his own reputation, is one which has had some notable exceptions. Furthermore, even scientists are by no means exempt from the temptation of seeking to use the threat system and even seeking to ally themselves with centers of political power in order to advance their own positions and their own theories. The Lysenko case in the Soviet

Union is perhaps the most scandalous, but no country has been immune to this kind of manipulation, and especially where science depends for its economic base on large government grants, the temptation to use political power to boost a personal theory becomes all the greater. It must be emphasized that these dialectical processes within science do not advance knowledge but retard it. Science does not progress by the conflicts of theories but by the testing of predictions. It does not progress by one theory conquering another in a revolution but rather by the slow growth of testable and tested images.

Social exchange

Another long cumulative process in a society which is essentially nondialectical is the process by which exchange develops the division of labor and increases human productivity. This process also has dialectical elements in it but the dialectical elements represent a minor disadvantage and a hindrance rather than an essential element of the process.

As we saw in Chapter 2, exchange has a strong tendency to be a positive-sum game in which both the parties benefit. If the exchange is uncoerced, that is, if there are no elements of the threat system involved in the decisions, it cannot take place at all unless *both* parties feel at the time of the decision to exchange that they will benefit. A person who thinks he will not benefit from an exchange can simply refuse to exchange, and the offer to exchange on the part of the first party will not be taken up. This still leaves open the possibility that in retrospect the exchange will turn out not to have been beneficial for one party or another. The goods we buy may turn out to be defective or we may decide we do not really want them after all. The money that we obtain from a sale may lose its value from inflation. The stock that we buy may fall in price, and we wish we had not bought it. Some of these disappointments are inevitable and arise out of unavoidable ignorance. Some of them may be the result of deception and cheating and can be safeguarded against to some extent by calling in the threat system of the law. Some disappointments again can be thought of as part of the cost of a learning process by which we learn to avoid some commodities and some exchanges and by which we learn to have more realistic expectations of the results of exchanges. In spite of these possible exceptions and because of the very learning process which they imply, the tendency for exchange to result in mutual benefit is overwhelmingly great in the long pull. This tendency is reinforced by opportunities for exchange, which promote the division of labor and specialization, and this in turn promotes an enormous increase in human productivity and welfare, in spite of certain human and social costs that are imposed by it. Without exchange, each family would be a Swiss Family Robinson, raising its own food, weaving its own cloth, building its own house, and providing its own amusement. The poverty of such a world would be beyond even that of the poorest peasant in India. Such, indeed, was the lot of paleolithic man, except in unusually favored spots.

The only dialectical element in exchange is the conflict which may take place in bilateral exchange about the *terms* of the bargain. If there is a range of prices in exchange at which both parties believe they will benefit the exchange will take place. Within this range, however, it is clear that the seller will prefer a high price and the buyer a low price. If the price is at the upper end of the range, most of the gains of the trade will go to the seller, but if it is at the lower end, most of the gain will go to the buyer.

Because this element of conflict in exchange is more visible than the positive sum and nonconflictual aspect of it, exchange has sometimes been misinterpreted as an essentially conflictual process. The conflict in exchange, however, is incidental to it and often does not occur at all. If it becomes acute, it can be destructive to the exchange process itself and can lead to a perverse dynamic process in which both parties become worse off instead of better off. The successful conduct of exchange requires that the parties to it have some sort of machinery for managing the conflict involved. If this machinery is inadequate, the inability to resolve the conflict may result in a loss for both parties, in that an exchange which would be beneficial for both of them on some terms does not take place at all because the terms cannot be agreed upon.

Here again, the dialectical process is a potentially destructive incident in what is essentially a nondialectical operation. Perhaps here it widens the term dialectical too much to make it include the conflict involved in bargaining. If we are to distinguish dialectical processes from conflict process in general, they must refer to conflicts in which the main issue is "who is the superior power." This, however, is a quite inappropriate model to describe the bargaining process. Bargaining power is not the power to destroy or supplant an opponent, but is the power to move to a more favorable position in which there is still a positive-sum game. If bargaining power is used dialectically, it destroys the whole process of bargaining. Bargaining power, furthermore, is a very strange phenomenon. It is often the weak who have the greater bargaining power, simply because the strong cannot afford to destroy the exchange relationship by pushing them to the wall. The whole concept of bargaining power, therefore, fits very badly into the dialectical framework of thought.

We see a good example of this in industrial relations. If the bargain between the employer and the worker is conceived in dialectical terms, that is, in terms of a class war in which one party or another must "win," the bargain will be in danger of breaking down altogether. The history of the labor movement in the United States provides an interesting example of this phenomena. The Industrial Workers of the

World (IWW) was a labor organization with a strong dialectical philosophy. It regarded the industrial relationship as a class war in which one party or the other had to win, and its object was to win this war and abolish the wage system. Because of this philosophy the organization virtually destroyed itself. It cast the industrial relationship in terms of a war which the union was bound to lose. It did lose, and its organization was almost destroyed. The "business unions," on the other hand, as represented by Gompers and the AFL (American Federation of Labor) rejected the dialectical view of the bargaining process. They did not set out to destroy the employers or to destroy the wage system but to get a good bargain. The AFL realized that bargaining implied co-existence, not class war, even though co-existence may not always be peaceful. This "business unionism" survived and flourished, whereas the labor organizations based on dialectical philosophy, whether the IWW or later the Communist-dominated unions doomed themselves to impotence and failure because they appraised an essentially nondialectical situation in dialectical terms.

When we look at the general process of economic development and technological and social invention, we find that this is also largely nondialectical. It occurs by a process of mutation and selection. Even though there is a conflict implied in the success of improved methods, between the new methods and the old less-productive ones, this may be thought of most fruitfully as a nondialectical conflict. It is a conflict like the famous Caucus race in Alice in Wonderland in which everybody wins and in which all must have prizes. Economic development is an essentially nonrevolutionary mutation-selection process. It is closely related to the process by which knowledge increases, and it is hardly an exaggeration to describe economic development simply as a particular aspect of the overall process of social learning. Even the process of accumulation of physical capital, which is an important aspect of economic development, must be interpreted primarily in terms of the imposition of a certain knowledge structure on the physical world. We do not get economic development by simply piling up stocks of old things. We do not get it, for instance, by simply accumulating big piles of wheat in warehouses. Rather, it consists in the development of new machines, tools, habits of behavior, and social organizations, all of which derive essentially from changes in knowledge. A machine is merely human knowledge imposed on the physical world.

Economic development

As in other nondialectical cumulative processes, economic development has a dialectical aspect. The displacement of the inferior by a superior method, for instance, is often accompanied by social conflicts and by a temporary worsening of the situation of those who cling to old methods. When a new, improved method first begins, it usually results in a substantial increase in output of the commodity affected, which results in a fall in its relative price. If the price did not fall, the users of the new methods would be too well off and would have terms of trade that were much too favorable. The new methods lower the cost of production, so that at the old price the users of the new method would have unusually high incomes. The fall in the price lowers the income of those who still cling to the old methods. A famous and tragic example of this process was the plight of the hand-loom weavers in England in the early days of the Industrial Revolution when the relative price of cloth fell sharply as the result of the introduction of machine methods. New methods also usually involve loss in the capital value of specialized capital invested in the old methods. Where this capital consists of human skill, the loss is particularly tragic. A man may find that a skill in which he has invested many years of his life suddenly becomes almost worthless. Even though economic development, like exchange, is a profoundly positive-sum process, in the sense that the gains far exceed the losses, for some people there are losses, and insofar as there are losses there is conflict.

The conflict, however, only becomes dialectical if it becomes involved in the threat system, that is, if the people who practice the older, less-efficient methods, attempt to adjust to the new situation, not by adapting themselves to the improved method but by defending the old one through invoking the threat system and the political power. It is at this point that dialectical processes may become relevant to economic development. The people who are in control of a state, for instance, may be a group of landlords who do well personally in spite of the poor techniques and low productivity of their tenants. Therefore, they resist technological improvement as a threat to their political power. Under circumstances such as this there may be a genuine revolutionary situation in which a shift in the locus of political power will release processes of development which bring eventual gain to all. One cannot rule out, therefore, the possibility of cases in which dialectical processes, such as war and revolution in which the challengers to existing power structures are successful, may speed up and release processes of economic development which have previously been suppressed.

Here we find again a curious paradox, that those revolutions which have been promoted and successfully carried out by those holding dialectical and revolutionary philosophies have been much less successful in promoting development than those revolutions and transfers of power which have taken place in a nondialectical setting. In Japan in 1868, for instance, and in Puerto Rico in 1941, there were shifts in power structure which set off a long cumulative process of economic development. One can even argue that the Glorious Revolution of 1688 in England was a similar shift. By contrast, the results of violent and dialectical revolutions have on the whole been disappointing. The French Revolution in 1783 led to a diversion of French energies to fruitless wars of conquest and slowed up the development of the French economy. The Russian revolution of 1917 led to an enormous waste of resources and disastrous internal conflict in the first collectivization; without a dialectical philosophy Russia would probably be much further along today. The nondialectical processes of cumulative growth in knowledge and technology, however, are so strong that they not only mask these dialectical interruptions, but the dialectical philosophies even get some credit for their achievements.

The integrative system

The integrative system, that is, the dynamic process by which human beings come to acquire love, respect, status, identity, identification, and so on, is so complex and so little understood that it is hard to say at present what is the mixture of dialectical and nondialectical processes within it. Insofar as it is part of the general learning process, the integrative system is basically nondialectical. If psychoanalysis has taught us anything it is that the dialectical processes in the family and especially between parents and children are most destructive to the integrative system. We have to learn to love and we likewise learn how to be incapable of love. The processes by which those learning processes are carried on are still obscure. Nevertheless, those who have been loved in childhood seem to have a much better chance of learning how to love in turn than those who have not been loved. When the dialectical processes of conflict and the war between the generations dominate the family situation, the children are more likely to grow up neurotic and alienated from the world, subject to mental and integrative disorders than they are in families where the dialectical processes, which are always present, are moderate and well controlled.

On a larger scale, as we have seen, integrative processes

in religions or ideologies tend to ally themselves with centers of threat systems, and then dialectical processes ensue between rival centers of integrative systems. The basic reason for this phenomenon is that threats have to be legitimated if they are to be effective as long-run organizers, and religions and ideological systems are very useful to the possessors of threat power because of their capacity to produce legitimation. The exponents of religious or ideological systems, therefore, often find support among "princes" who wish to legitimate their own counterthreat system to some rival center of power. Thus, the spread of ideological systems is forced into the pattern of the threat system and adopts a dialectical dynamics. The success and power of a center of threat power depends in large measure on its ability to involve a successful ideology or integrative organizer. Thus, we see the Christian church, in its early days, as a rival integrative system to the Roman Empire, which eventually was absorbed into the Empire under Constantine. Islam provided an integrative structure for the Arabs and the Arab conquests. The long dialectical process between Christianity and Islam is much more a reflection of the fact that they legitimated complexes of political threat than of anything inherent in the ideologies themselves. In our own day we see Marxism as a new Islam legitimating and organizing another complex of threat systems. Again, we find that the centers of threat use competing ideologies to justify themselves in a split, as for instance between Moscow and Peking.

On the whole I am inclined to regard these dialectical elements in the integrative system as symptoms of disease rather than of health. It is true that one of the easiest ways of achieving an integrative system is by combining people against a common enemy. A common fear and common hatred is a great integrator, and a nation realizes a high degree of internal integration in external war. This is an integration on a small scale which is achieved at the cost of a disintegration on a large scale. It is a precarious source of integration even on a small scale. A sect or a nation may seek to maintain its internal unity by fomenting a mutual hatred against an external enemy. Once hatred is generated, however, it can be turned inward almost as easily as it can be turned outward, and those organizations and societies which have sought integration in this way have often found themselves later pulled apart by internal factions, dissensions, splits, and civil wars. The hatred of an external enemy, whether it is in a person or in a nation, is often a symptom of a deep internal self-hatred which is a symptom of a failure to solve the problem of integration and identification within.

It seems reasonable, therefore, to attribute the process by which a man learns to identify himself with others and eventually with all mankind as a cumulative nondialectical process somewhat akin to the process of the growth of knowledge. This does not exclude the possibility of real dialectical processes with the integrative system. Sometimes status has to be denied and respect has to be withdrawn when those who stand high within an existing integrative system do so because of some past condition which no longer reflects the reality of the present or the future. The integrative system exhibits long lags, and if we bestow excessive love and respect and, one might add, excessive hatred and disrespect on those who are not worthy of either, the system will exhibit inner contradictions in which can easily give rise to a dialectical process. In this respect, an integrative system oddly enough follows some of the patterns of the threat system. The ability to command love, like the ability to command fear, diminishes with distance. These relationships, however, are very complex. Sometimes indeed, distance lends enchantment to the view, and absence makes the heart grow fonder. At other times, not only is "out of sight, out of mind" but out of heart, too. The possibility of genuine dialectical processes, akin to those of the threat system but independent of them, arising in the integrative structure should not be overlooked. Nevertheless, it would probably be a great mistake to make these dialectical processes central in the dynamics of the integrative system, for they seem nearly always to be self-defeating and to block that long painfully slow process by which we are growing to a genuinely integrative system for mankind as a whole, a process in which no man or woman shall be an alien either to himself or to others.

In considering these various cases, a single theme of great importance has emerged. Even though the fundamental processes both of biological and social evolution are primarily nondialectical, dialectical processes do occur within them. These are often adverse to the values that we think of as being embodied in progress, so that one is tempted at times to identify the dialectical with the unprogressive. There are rare occasions on which this is reversed, and the dialectical process indeed is an instrument of progress. This leads to the conclusion that even though dialectical processes are occasionally progressive, the dialectical philosophy is almost invariably unprogressive, that is, the dialectical philosophy in itself is likely to lead to bad judgments about reality, to the misinterpretation of actual situations, and to distortions which hinder the genuinely nondialectical progressive forces of history. By the dialectical philosophy I mean all those ideologies which regard conflict as the essential process in development and therefore tend to put a high intrinsic value on conflict, struggle, war, and revolution.

The two principal examples of dialectical philosophy today are militant Nationalism and Marxist Communism. The adherents of these philosophies tend to interpret all situations as dialectical whether they are so in fact or not. Insofar as actual dialectical situations are rare, dialectical philosophies will lead to a high proportion of bad decisions. One can see, for instance, how a dialectical philosophy of nationalism led the rulers of Japan into some disastrous decisions between 1937 and 1941. One can see how dialectical philosophy led to some disastrous decisions in the socialist countries, such as the first collectivization in the Soviet Union, or the "great leap forward" in the People's Republic of China. It is equally true that the absence of *any* philosophy of history can lead to equally disastrous decisions or failure to decide, such as those characterized by the great depression in the United States in 1929 to 1932, or the incompetence of the western powers in the 1930's. Whether a dialectical philosophy of history is better than no philosophy would make a nice point for debate! This is an unreal dilemma, the solution for which is the search for better philosophies of history.

Developmental philosophy

Such a philosophy is now emerging from the work of many thinkers. We may call it perhaps "the developmental philosophy." It is a view of history which recognizes both dialectical and nondialectical elements in the historical process. It, consequently, is able to assess each situation in which decision has to be made with more freedom and more realism than those people enjoy who are committed to a narrower view. It is a view of the historical process which has emerged out of the epistemological processes of science. Its basic concept is that of testing, not that of conflict. The success of the scientific enterprise has been a result of a view of the growth of knowledge which lays stress on the specific testing of particular propositions, not on the dialectical conflict of systems or of political and social organizations. In the pre-scientific age, man's view of the world was essentially ideological. These ideologies served to provide the basis for the integrative structure and the organization of separate societies, and the conflict among these societies largely determined the spread of the various ideologies. There was a testing process in all this, in the sense that societies which believed less nonsense had a better chance of surviving in this conflict than societies which believed more nonsense. What survived, however, was the total ideological package containing both sense and nonsense. The peculiar genius of the nondialectical revolution of science has been the discovery of a way of increasing knowledge by separating out the components of ideological packages and testing individual propositions separately. The growth of knowledge, then, no longer depends on dialectical conflicts of total systems in which one system overcomes another, but on the testing of individual propositions and the gradual adjustments of the total systems as individual propositions succeed or fail in the testing process.

What we are now witnessing, one hopes, is the extension of the scientific as opposed to the ideological point of view into the developmental processes of man and his societies. This is the essence of the developmental philosophy. The testing process is by no means easy. The arbitration of the threat system, for instance, still determines in considerable part whether society shall be essentially a planned economy or shall be a guided market economy. The fate of Czechoslovakia or Vietnam or Cuba or Santo Domingo are being determined by dialectical not by scientific processes. In spite of the destructiveness of these dialectical processes, the developmental processes go on. For instance, both the socialist and the capitalist world are slowly being transformed from within by the slow growth of the social sciences. For individual persons and societies, of course, dialectical processes are highly relevant, but for the historical process of mankind they are relatively insignificant. Once this is perceived, the dialectical processes themselves will be transformed into processes which are closer to the principles of direct and specific testing, which is the only foundation for secure advances in knowledge and in welfare.

CHAPTER 5

THE MARXIST DIALECTIC

The two most important dialectical images of the world, both of which exercise enormous influence on the minds of men today, are Marxism and Nationalism. Nationalism is a state of mind belonging to the realm of folk images and hardly deserves the title of a philosophy of history. Marxism, however, is another matter. This is explicitly a dialectical philosophy of history, designed to give to its adherents a sense that they hold the key not only to the past but to the future. If this key is, as I believe, a rusty one, capable of opening only a few locks, the existence of a large number of people who hold this view is an obstacle to the realization of that reasonably happy future for mankind which the developmental philosophy envisages as possible. It is important, therefore, to examine Marxism to see in the first place what we can learn from it, which is a good deal, and in the second place to see how its propositions may perhaps be removed from the realm of ideological conflict, which cannot by its very nature test their truth, into the realm of testing.

Marxist philosophy is elaborate and has an enormous literature, and it would be presumptuous even to attempt a complete summary in a single chapter. I will, therefore, neglect the Marxist theory of relative prices, which finally turned out to be a discounted, embodied labor theory not very different from that of Ricardo. This Marxist theory is acceptable enough to modern economists as a special case under some circumstances, but is likely to get us into serious misconceptions where the labor force is not the major element limiting production. I also propose to skip over his theories of unemployment and depression which are not very different from those of Malthus and, with a somewhat kindly interpretation, anticipate in a rather unclear way the discoveries of Keynes. Marx's economic writings are seriously marred by some fundamental confusions of dimensions as between stock concepts and flow concepts which also characterize his predecessors of the English Classical School. As a pure economist, therefore, Marx can not be said to have advanced our understanding much beyond where Ricardo and Malthus left it. The great developments of modern economics really came after him and owe little to him. I propose, therefore, to confine myself to two major aspects of his thought: the theory of dialectical materialism as an interpretation of history and the theory of surplus value which is indeed the key to his total system.

Dialectical materialism

It was his followers rather than Marx who called his system dialectical materialism. Nevertheless it did take over from Hegel the notion of the dialectical process as a succession of systems through contradiction and conflict as the essential process of history, with the amendment ("Standing Hegel on his head") that it was the material conditions of production rather than the spirit, that is, the ideas and conscious mental processes, which were the essential systems which governed the process. Both Marx and Engels undoubtedly thought of themselves as materialists and believed that this indeed constituted their major contribution to the theory of dialectical processes. In part, their materialism was a protest against religion. Both of them were militant atheists, and hostile even towards agnosticism. In part, their materialism can be seen as a descendent of the eighteenth century "enlightenment" of Voltaire and Rousseau.

There is a paradox here in the sense that philosophical materialism, meaning by this the doctrine that matter is the only reality and that mental phenomena are mere by-products of some complex physical and chemical process, is not really consistent with Marx's concept of production as the major social reality. Production refers to the production of commodities, and a commodity is not an arrangement of matter but is a relation between an arrangement of matter and a mental image. Ice at the North Pole is not a commodity, but ice in the ice house is. The difference between these two objects consists not in their material, physical, or chemical composition, which is identical, but in their wantedness and scarcity, both of which are properties of mind rather than of matter. The philosophical question whether the properties of mind are in effect merely dependent upon properties of some kind of material system is irrelevant, for whether this is true or not we do not know how to describe such complex material systems. The description has to be limited to describing the mental properties as such. The very concept of production, therefore, on which Marx sets such great importance, is essentially dependent upon the properties of the mental world, that is, a function of man's consciousness.

The problem of philosophical materialism, then, is irrelevant to the more fundamental question of the Marxian system which is whether it is in fact the conditions of production and particularly what he called the relations of production, that is the social institutions under which production is carried out, that primarily determine the course of history and constitute the systems between which dialectical interaction takes place. Indeed, even if one does not believe in dialectics or if one thinks, as I do, that dialectical processes are only a small part, and often a somewhat retrogressive part, of the more fundamental nondialectical processes of history, one could still hold that the conditions and relations of production played an important role in the historical and developmental process.

Surplus value

The concept of surplus value is so fundamental to the Marxist system that we cannot go much further without coming to grips with it. The basic concept is simple and is indeed a sound one which comes essentially from Adam Smith. *Surplus value* may be defined as the excess of the total production of commodities over that minimum quantity of commodities which must be consumed in the course of producing the amount produced. This bare minimum of necessary consumption is what is usually known as subsistence. Surplus value, therefore, is the excess of total production over subsistence. Marx, then, sees history as largely the record of the struggle for surplus value, this being in a sense all that is available to struggle over. The worker, or whoever does the production, has to be given subsistence or no production will result. If there is any excess over subsistence, however, the possibility arises that somebody may appropriate it. Then the question of who controls the surplus value, that is, the available excess of commodities, is the key to the history and development of society. It is

Marx's prime contention that the owner of the means of production controls surplus value.

This is a description which fits the pattern of what might be called classical civilization fairly well. In a paleolithic society, there is no surplus value. It takes the hunter and fisher all his time and energy to produce enough food for his own family. If production rises temporarily above subsistence then the population soon rises until it is back to the subsistence level again. *Subsistence* must be defined as that quantity and kinds of production which will just permit the population to sustain itself and reproduce itself. Surplus value on any scale appears only with the development of agriculture. In some neolithic villages (Marx's *primitive communism*), the surplus seems to have been controlled by the community as a whole and fairly evenly distributed. Civilization and the urban revolution arise as we saw earlier with the development of an organized threat system which can take excess food production away from the food producer and with it feed the armies and artisans that surround the king or the court. A dialectical process then begins because it is virtually impossible to prevent new centers of power from arising and competing with the old.

Marx was more interested in the succession of classes than he was in the succession of empires. For all the importance that he gave to the concept of class, he never seems to have analyzed it very carefully. For his purposes a crude concept was no doubt sufficient. The simple model of a king or a lord extracting surplus value from agricultural laborers by threats and using it to maintain the threat system as well as to enjoy himself with any surplus that was left over afterwards, is perhaps a caricature, but certainly a recognizable caricature not only of early civilization but also of the feudal estate. In Marx's eyes, organized religion is simply a part of a threat system, designed to keep surplus value flowing from the producers of commodities by means of spiritual rather than physical threats. This again is a caricature which is not wholly unrecognizable. The first break in the system comes with the development of a merchant class and towns with a bourgeoisie. This comes about mainly because of the development of specialization and trade which introduced a new form of property—goods in transit and goods in stock. The development of bills, debts, and financial instruments and the increasing of the use of money also leads to a class of money lenders and financiers whose property is in this form. The bourgeoisie is sometimes able to create a new center of political power and a threat system of its own and set itself up in independent cities like those of the Hanseatic League. In a sense, this represents the first "class revolution," the replacement of the king and the landed aristocracy by the ruling bourgeoisie. The power of the bourgeoisie is strengthened still further by the development of machine technology, for this introduces another new form of capital and property distinct from aristocratic land ownership and leads to a full-fledged system of capitalism. It is characterized by private property in the means of production and the dominance of the state (a committee of the bourgeoisie) by the owners of industrial and commercial property.

In the meantime the third class is beginning to arise. This is the working class, the source of all products, on whose back the structure has been built. Because the working class has been gathered into factories, it is able to organize, to achieve social self-consciousness through reading the works of Marx, and eventually to organize the second revolution which raises it to dominance. The capitalists are overthrown, their property is expropriated, and a party of self-appointed representatives of the working class govern the society on their behalf. Then in some mysterious fashion, which is never explained, the state is supposed to wither away, as presumably there is plenty for everybody, and no threat system is needed any more to take anything away from anyone.

Figure 6 illustrates the pattern of the Marxian dynamic. Time is measured from left to right. AB is a preagricultural society with production just about equal to subsistence and no surplus value. Anything above the dotted line is surplus value. From B to C we have early agriculture and primitive

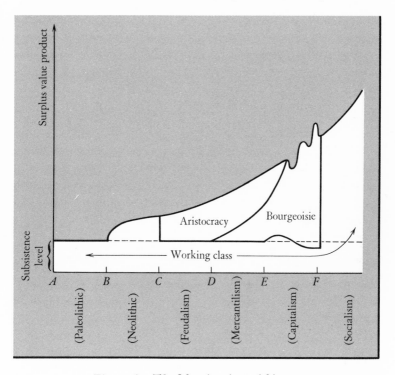

Figure 6.   The Marxist view of history

communism with surplus value rising but fairly equally distributed with no classes. At C we get the urban revolution and a separation into an upper and lower class, the lower class retaining its subsistence, the upper class enjoying surplus value. From D to E we get the rise of the bourgeoisie, and at E comes a bourgeois revolution at which the aristocrats are either eliminated or forcibly amalgamated with the bourgeois group. Then from E to F the power of the working class gradually rises, although by some strange processes it is also supposed to be getting more oppressed, and miserable until finally at F there is the proletarian revolution. The bourgeoisie is in turn eliminated, and the worker state or dictatorship of the proletariat ensues from F on. This is the end of the process as there are no other classes to arise.

Again as a caricature of history, this is not unrecognizable. It is, however, in many ways a dangerous caricature, for anybody who takes it for reality itself may get into serious trouble. First, Marx's theory of production is seriously deficient. He regards production only as the result of acts of labor, and commodities as embodying labor as a kind of mystical substance. A commodity is for Marx a "jelly of embodied labor time," and not even a jelly of real labor time but of some "socially necessary" labor time. The latter is to take account of the fact that merely putting labor into something does not make it a commodity if nobody wants it. In all this, there is no organization and no motivation. Production seems to be something that is supposed to happen by people spontaneously putting a hand to a plough which somebody else has previously and spontaneously made. Capital is simply embodied labor, and labor, one supposes, is simply disembodied commodities. This peculiar mystical-mechanical process is almost as far from the real world as one can get.

It is this deficiency in the theory of production which makes the basic ethical proposition of Marxism invalid. The ethical proposition is that because labor made everything, labor should get everything, or at least, nearly everything. The idea of the total product as, in some sense, wholly the product of labor predates Marx, but it was he who erected this doctrine into what is almost a new religion.

It is a dirty dialectical trick to turn Marx upside down, which is what *he* thought he was doing to Hegel! We can say, for instance, that labor produces nothing. Labor is simply an incoherent potential, just as ore in the ground or coal in the mine is incoherent potential. Neither labor nor coal produce anything until they are organized into a process of production. It is *organization* that is the real producer, not labor. Who, however, is the organizer? Why—none other than the capitalist; he who owns, and by his owner-ship, ultimately controls the means of production. Capital, therefore, produces everything, and insofar as the working class extorts more than its subsistence from the capitalists, labor is exploiting capital! Marx on his head perhaps sounds pretty silly, but he is really not much sillier than Marx on his feet.

The fact is that the process of production is essentially an organizational process, not a mechanical process of adding bits of labor to bits of embodied labor. It is also a process of extreme complexity to which all persons and all institutions contribute in some degree positively or negatively. There is nothing automatic about it, as countries like Indonesia, which have neglected the process of production, are finding out to their cost. The communist countries themselves, once they have gotten into the business of economic development, have had to violate many of their own principles and have had to introduce elaborate organization, a crude price system, wide income differentials, and even, out of the sheer logic of rational planning, something that looks like a rate of interest.

Theory of distribution

The second weakness of the Marxian system is the absence of an adequate theory of distribution. In this respect, Marx merely fails to improve on the classical economists who also did not have an adequate theory of distribution.

Even today, there are some quite serious unsolved economic problems in this regard. Marx, adopted a specific subsistence theory of wages which assumed in effect that nearly all surplus value would remain in the hands of the capitalists. He envisages, then, the process of capital accumulation and technological development as one in which wages remained at the subsistence level but the income of the capitalist continually grew. His picture of the economic process we show in Figure 7. Time is again measured from left to right and national income vertically. TT' shows the rise in total capacity income with economic development and capital accumulation. PP' shows actual product, with increasing fluctuations and unemployment. WW' shows labor income remaining at subsistence so that the proportion of

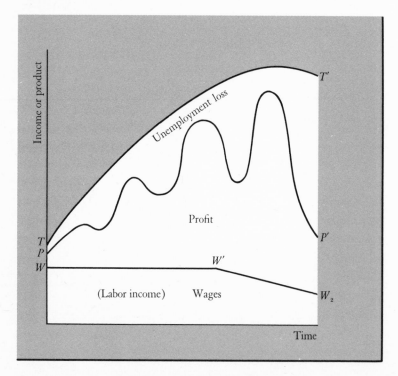

Figure 7. The Marxist dynamic

income going into wages continually declines. In fact, he supposed a situation even worse than this. Because the capitalists cannot consume and invest *all* their gross income, after a certain time production begins to decline because of unemployment, and wages go down to W_2, not only because of unemployment but because of the competition of the unemployed, and things go from bad to worse.

What has happened in the successfully developing capitalist societies such as the United States, Western Europe, and Japan, as shown in Figure 8, is that the proportion of national income going to labor has remained either fairly stable or has risen slowly. The proportion going to property income has declined slowly, and surplus value has been widely distributed to the working class, even to those who

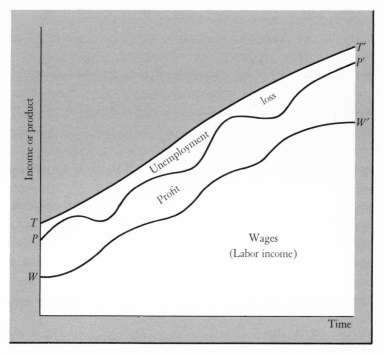

Figure 8. The developmental dynamic

played very little part in creating it, outside of doing what they were told and what they were paid to do. The exact process by which surplus value has been so widely distributed is not clear. Part of it is the result of the operation of the forces of the market themselves which have continually raised real wages in a developing society, part of it has been the development of a "grants economy" involving social security, unemployment insurance, pensions and so on. Whatever the reason, the fact remains that the dynamics of at least the successful capitalist societies have followed an entirely different course from that which Marx predicted.

The remarkable stability of the distributional shares for the last forty years in the United States is shown in Figure 9 where we see the distribution of national income among its various components. Apart from the disappearance of

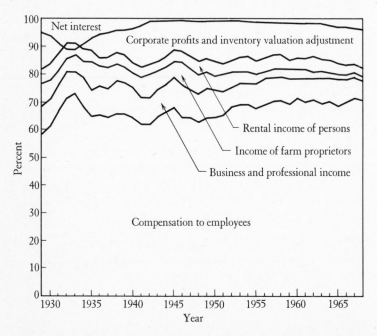

Figure 9. Components of national income as a percentage of national income

profits in the Great Depression, the proportional shares have been remarkably stable with a slight upward trend in labor income as opposed to property income. From the National Income Statistics, it is not possible to differentiate the proportion going to labor and the proportion going to property. However, if we suppose that the great part of farm income and income from professions and unincorporated business is in fact labor income, as it is likely to be, the total labor income is close to 80 percent and property income is about 20 percent. The distribution by functional shares does not tell us what the personal distribution of income is like, but this also does not seem to have changed very much in the last two or three decades.

My personal view is that we have not redistributed enough from the rich to the poor in the United States and that we could do much better. Social democracy indeed has seen far too much of subsidizing the rich in the name of helping the poor, and we need to reexamine our whole structure of grants and redistributions in the light of who really gets them. Labor income in the United States, however, rises in about four or five years of average growth by as much as the whole amount of property income. Under these circumstances, the attempt to destroy property income or to redistribute it to labor income, which would almost certainly destroy the process of growth itself, would seem absurdly costly. It is not surprising that the United States does not represent a revolutionary situation.

In fact, the dynamics of the communist societies is much closer to that of Marx's view of capitalism. In the Soviet Union, for instance, real wages have been held down or even have declined over long periods, and it took nearly thirty years after the revolution for them to get back to the 1913 pre-revolutionary level. Meanwhile, surplus value continues to accumulate in the hands of the state and in the control of the party elite. This is beginning to change now and it may well be that under a more moderate regime the Soviet Union will repeat the capitalistic experience, and even in a communist society surplus value may be distributed to the working class.

This leads to what I have called "the doctrine of the missed bus." This is the view that in the course of economic development there is, a "moment" for socialism. In the early stages of economic development, the pattern looks much more like the Marxian model. Where the country still has a large peasant or even feudal rural sector, economic development can easily result in the increase of surplus value falling wholly into the hands of a small class of capitalists and landowners. The early stages of economic development almost always result in increasing inequality of income, if only because a society can rarely develop uniformly. If one part of society develops while the rest does not, the part that develops will grow ahead of the rest, increasing its income, while the rest stagnates, or even perhaps goes downhill a little as the traditional sector finds itself in competition with the advanced sector. At this moment, the bus for socialism comes along and Marxism looks plausible. It is easy to whip up hatred against the rich, and if the existing regime is incompetent or unpopular and especially if it gets involved in an unsuccessful war, a revolutionary overthrow may be achieved and a communist party gets into power. The country then rides off in the socialist bus, and it is hard to get off it.

Sometimes, however, the moment for socialism passes. In Western Europe the moment was probably 1848 and it was too early. The Communist Manifesto had just been written, and there was no organized communist party anywhere which could take advantage of the discontent and disturbance and affect revolutionary overthrow. Once the moment has passed and the bus has gone by, if there is a successful process of capitalist development, the Marxist system becomes increasingly unrealistic and the socialist alternative increasingly unattractive. It is one thing to cry "workers of the world unite, you have nothing to lose but your chains"; it is another to urge the workers of the world to "unite for you have nothing to lose but your outboard motors." A long run rise in real wages is poor fuel for the revolutionary fire. In the United States I doubt if the socialist bus *ever* came by, although there was a moment in 1932 when it might have been glimpsed somewhere down the street. One of the things which contributes to the instability of the present world is that for a great many precapitalist countries the bus has not come by yet, and the question is still open as to which mode of development they wish to follow.

Another aspect of Marx's social theory which illustrates his capacity for giving the wrong answer to the right question is his theory of alienation. Marx's views on alienation may owe something to the fact that he was a Jew, for the Jews are a people called by their God, even when they do not believe in him, to be aliens in this world. The great and disproportionate contribution of the Jews to human development arises, indeed, in no small measure from this characteristic. Only the alienated can change society. Marx perceived clearly that the process of industrialization involved the breakup of old social and traditional relationships, and this could easily create in the industrial worker a sense of alienation from his own society. Here, perhaps, Marx tended to cast the mantle of his own experience over the whole of society, for not only was he a Jew but for the most of his life he was an alien and an exile in a strange land. Nevertheless, though the problem he raises is real, even if he exaggerated it, his image of the worker as finding his citizenship as it were in the class war and his identification with the working class has turned out to be unrealistic. In the integrative system, the forces of nationalism have proved much stronger than the forces of class. Not only was this true in the nineteenth century and in the first world war when the socialist working class set about killing each other with just about as much enthusiasm as the Christians, but we see now in the present breakup of the socialist camp that when it comes to the integrative system on a world scale, even among the socialists, nationalism is much stronger than allegiance to a common ideology. In the search for identity (the opposite of alienation), it is the national group which seems to exert the strongest pull.

Dialectical conflict, therefore, is much more likely to take the form of international war than it is to take the form of class war. The unity of the working class is a myth. Where there have been class wars, as in the first collectivization in the Soviet Union which resulted in the extermination of the Kulaks, the war had to be whipped up by a reign of furious internal propaganda and terror and winning it proved to be enormously costly to the victors. Even to this day, the Soviet Union has not recovered from the loss of some five million of its best farmers and over half of its livestock. The class wars in Hungary, in East Germany, and in Cuba have been fomented by a small group of ideologues and have resulted in the exile of many thousands of able people in each country. Here again the winning of a class war has resulted in a serious economic loss to the victors.

We shall not understand the appeal of Marxism or its strength unless we recognize that in spite of the weakness of its social theory and the fact that it represents a fixation on a midnineteenth century social science hopelessly inadequate for the modern world, Marxism nevertheless represents an ethical challenge. As a social scientist, Marx is outdated. As a prophet and as an ethical preacher he still has something to say to us. The labor theory of value and what might be called the labor theory of production may be poor social science but one can see its appeal to those who see people in a society receiving income for which they seem to perform no function. The idle rich represents a cost rather than an asset to society, and a class of functionless consumers cannot comfortably be regarded as a social asset. Oddly enough, it is harder to justify the existence of a small upper class in a rich than in a poor society where, if income were distributed evenly, all would descend to a uniform level of misery and no high achievement of any kind would be possible. The critical question is whether the cost of getting rid of the rich is greater or less than the cost of putting up with them, particularly when the institutions which produce them also produce rapid economic development and wide distribution of surplus value. It has become clear that we do not get rid of poverty by redistributing income but by increasing the total. When, in the United States, consumption by the idle rich probably amounts to less than five percent of the national income, this hardly seems worth a revolutionary upheaval to get rid of. The real problem is on its way to solution by an essentially nondialectical process.

Similarly, in regard to alienation and the integrative system, Marx turned out to be wrong not only about nationalism but also about religion. Marx became fixated on an adolescent revolt against his Lutheran high school. Communism became identified with atheism, which is really irrelevant to the question as to whether economic development is best carried out by a market economy or by a centrally planned society. The evidence suggests that religion does not tend to disappear in a developed society, and it indeed becomes an essential element in the disalienation of industrialized man, providing him sociologically with a moral community which is a necessary substitute for the small geographical community of the villages which he has lost forever. Where the church allies itself with an existing power structure, in effect it commits itself to a dialectical process, and Marx's criticism has some justification. By his atheism, however, Marx put himself squarely on one side of an irrelevant battle, and on the side which is by no means sure of ultimate victory. Nevertheless, Marx's rage was not altogether in vain, and his attacks may have played some part in arousing the Christian church in particular, and perhaps also the Buddhist, to a greater awareness of the social system in which it is placed.

Marx is one of the people after whom the world is never quite the same again. Nevertheless, the human misery which has been caused, however indirectly, by Marxism is so enormous and the tyranny which it has fostered is so monstrous, the corruption of not only art and literature, architecture and even science which Marxist society suffered is so painful; and what is even worse the corruption of simple human friendship and all the ordinary decencies of life which is so typical of communism is so terrifying, that one wonders how a movement which originated from a genuine and deep moral protest and from a deeply moral man could possibly have led to so much misery.

Dialectical philosophy

The principal villain would seem to be the dialectical philosophy. This places a premium on conflicts even where they might be avoided, it provides a magnificent excuse for the expression of aggression and hatred, and it diverts attention from the solutions of problems to the winning of victories. It is to the credit of Marx that he was one of the first to recognize that mankind in this period is passing through a very profound transition and that indeed a new world is coming into being which, whether we like it or not, is going to be very different from the old. In a very real sense, history is coming to an end, in the sense of the record of wars and empires, revolutions and class struggles, all arising out of competition for the pitiful fragment of surplus value which is all that preindustrial techniques permitted. It is possible that the human race will not make this transition and that it will either destroy itself entirely or fall back into barbarism. It cannot stay where it is; it must either go on into a very new kind of society or it will fall back. But this is not a dialectical process. It is not a process in which somebody wins and somebody loses, but a process of slow cumulative change. The attempt to interpret this process in dialectical terms is not only unrealistic, it could easily set it back.

Both in the Soviet Union and China one can see how many times the dialectical philosophy interfered with the processes of economic development and resulted in costly mistakes in policy. In the Soviet Union (Lenin's war) communism created a major famine and almost destroyed industrial production. The civil war can be blamed for some of it, but not all of it. Lenin himself was wise enough to be a revisionist, that is, someone who can learn from experience, and he accordingly revised his policies drastically in the New Economic Policy, which called something of a halt to the class war and permitted limited private trade. Under this less dialectical regime, there was a remarkable economic recovery until 1928 when the dialectic took over again in the first five-year plan and the first collectivization of agriculture. A ruthless class war was stirred up in the villages which resulted in the death of some five million people and the crippling of Russian agriculture. In the Thirties, the revolution turned on itself and consumed many of its distinguished children in the "purges." The Soviet Union is now in a less dialectical period, but still the legacy of class war, especially in agriculture, is a grim one.

China is attempting a development based essentially on a war psychology. Here again problem solving has gone out of the window and disastrous mistakes in planning, such as the "great leap forward," which cost China at least three of four years, and perhaps a decade, of economic growth, is evidence of the further deplorable consequences of dialectical thinking.

Even the United States is not immune, for the language it uses in the cold war is the language of dialectics. Even in internal policy, President Johnson evidently regarded poverty as an enemy to be fought rather than as a problem to be solved. Everywhere indeed one can see dialectical thinking getting in the way of solving problems. Indonesia and Cuba are again highly revolutionary countries with revolutionary ideologies, where economic development for some years actually went into reverse and per capita incomes declined, mainly because a revolutionary ideology is better adapted to the winning of fights than to the solution of problems. Economic development, however, is not a fight but a problem, and a revolutionary ideology is a severe handicap in facing it. Revolution is like a conception. This is perhaps why it is so often associated with an exaggerated masculinity, such as the "masculinismo" which has cursed the history of Latin America. Development, however, is more like the growth of a child in the womb. It requires a nondialectical continuous cumulative process, and the revolutionary philosophy does nothing to help it.

There are only two points at which I can see the dialectical philosophy, especially in communism, assisting the process of economic development. A dialectical philosophy may result in a willingness to sacrifice brutally one whole generation in the supposed interests of its descendents. This, however, is a gross violation of social justice, for it is unjust that one generation should be asked to bear the whole cost of rapid development.

The second point at which dialectical philosophy might assist economic development is in situations where the power structure in a nondeveloping or slowly developing society cannot be overthrown except by revolutionary means. Revolution in this case is something like the "shock treatment" of a mentally sick patient; it achieves a disruption of the old, pathological organization and hence opens up the possibility of a reorganization along more developmental lines. This nearly always requires a "second revolution," or the replacement of the old revolutionaries by a less revolutionary, more developmental type of leader. The worst thing is a perpetual revolution—a patient always under shock. Furthermore, just as shock treatment has become old-fashioned and is now used by the most advanced therapists only as a last resort, so we may expect a process of political maturation by which we learn to achieve nonrevolutionary transformations to a developing society.

The impact of Marxism provides another excellent example of a proposition which we have developed several times, that dialectical processes are more successful when they are imbedded in a large nondialectical matrix. In the internal policies of countries of Western Europe, the United States, the British Commonwealth, and Japan the impact of Marxism has been largely beneficial. It has performed a function of valuable social criticism, it has aroused the social conscience, and it has resulted in a long nondialectical process of economic change. The working class has slowly been integrated into the structure of society through public education, the labor movement, and political democracy. Economic development has reduced the proletariat to a small minority, and while Utopia is still a long way off, at least most of the members of this generation are considerably better off than their grandparents. The great weakness of the West has been its inability to conduct international relations except on a dialectical basis. Here the dialectical element of its own social system has almost proved its undoing.

The socialist countries, as long as they are in the dialectical and revolutionary phase, develop at an enormously high cost in terms of human suffering and corruption. The most hopeful sign of the times is that we may be moving towards a nondialectical socialism in these countries with more personal, political, religious, and scientific liberty and a shift from an ideology of struggle to an ideology of problem solving, even though lip service still has to be paid to dialectical materialism. One has some hope, therefore, that the question as to the role of the market and of central planning in economic organization may eventually be removed from its present ideological and dialectical framework and be submitted to the same processes of rational discussion and testing which characterizes the spirit of the scientific method. I have elsewhere characterized Marxism as "folk science." It is the kind of view of the world which goes beyond unsophisticated folk images derived from personal experience, in the sense that it does attempt to draw inferences from theories rather than from mere observations. Engels incidently, in his famous attack on spiritualism, had a very acute perception of science as drawing its inferences from a consistent logical theoretical view of the world and not from mere instances and experiences. The weakness of Marxism lies in the absence of any adequate testing of the theories and images and inferences derived from them, perhaps because of the emotional commitment to the ideology. A true science must be revisionist, that is, it must revise its image of the world in the light of the testing of predictions made from it. As the Chinese see so clearly Marxism can hardly be revisionist without ceasing to be Marxism. Perhaps we are not too far from the time when ideology can lay down its life in the interest of knowledge.

CHAPTER 6

REVOLUTIONISM

One aspect of the dialectical philosophy which is worth special attention is what might be called *revolutionism*. This is the doctrine which places a high value on revolution as a social phenomenon in itself, which puts a high value on the revolutionary spirit, and which looks back to the past revolutions as shining examples of how man ought to behave. Of all the manifestations of the dialectical philosophy this seems to me the most sentimental and the one which has the highest social cost. It is the one which is most likely to frustrate development.

As I pointed out earlier, the term *revolution* is used to describe two quite different phenomena. I myself have been guilty of this confusion of terms. I once wrote a book called *The Organizational Revolution*. Terms, such as the industrial revolution, managerial revolution, even the Copernican revolution, and the Keynesian revolution, are descriptive of what mathematicians might call the second differentials of history, that is, they are changes in the rate of change. If we want to invent a new word to describe them, perhaps the term *accelerations* is the best word, for a period of acceleration is one in which the rate of change increases. Sometimes the acceleration continues over a considerable period. Sometimes we have a sudden acceleration where the acceleration itself soon stops but is followed by a period of higher rate of change. This concept is illustrated in Figure 10. If *ABC*

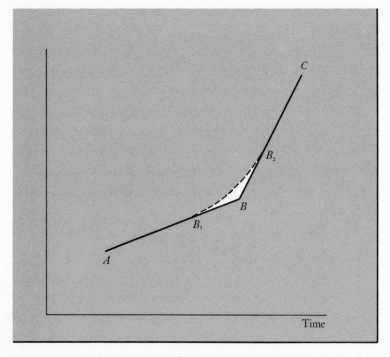

Figure 10. The dynamics of an acceleration

represents some process of development over time with one rate of change for *A* to *B* and higher rate of change from *B* to *C,* then the point *B* represents an acceleration. Sometimes the acceleration takes places over a period of time as from

B_1 to B_2, sometimes it takes place rather suddenly as at B. In either case the fundamental phenomenon of acceleration is similar.

Measurements of change

I have deliberately avoided the question of what it is that accelerates, that is, what is the vertical axis in Figure 10 or what is the measure of development. An economist has fairly easy answers to these questions in terms of such concepts as the gross national product per capita, or more accurately, disposable personable income per capita, all of which are rough measures of the process of economic development. These measures are open to criticism even as measures of economic welfare. The gross national product, can increase for purely statistical reasons as when household production, which was not counted before, is replaced by industrial production, which is counted. It may increase because of an expansion of the war industry which is a result of the international dialectical process and does not usually contribute much to economic welfare. The gross national product also is concerned primarily with the level of production in society which is necessary to replace what is consumed and to add to the total stock. Within the same gross national product, therefore, an increase in consumption which is nonproductive of human welfare such as commuting, the correction of environmental pollution, conspicuous waste, and so on, will change the significance of the gross national product figure. When we try to assess things as the quality of human life or the esthetic and cultural qualities of the society, the measure of development becomes more difficult and the concept of development becomes vague.

This difficulty of measurement is not trivial. If it were total, the whole concept of development would break down because we cannot promote a development that we cannot recognize or promote an acceleration when we do not know what is being accelerated. There may be a real conflict of values here which is not easy to resolve. If a man says he would rather be poor under socialism than rich under capitalism, this is his privilege of choice, and one would like to see a world indeed in which this choice can be expressed through having a variety of types of societies within which people can move freely. When all of these qualifications have been made, however, economic measures of development, perhaps only because they are the best that we have, retain a significance provided one recognizes their limitations.

Revolution in the sense of political upheaval usually accompanied by violence, in which an existing class or clique of rulers is displaced by another, is almost invariably an interruption of the process of development. A successful revolution, such as is illustrated in Figure 11, results in a higher rate of change afterwards, that is, it is combined with an acceleration, but the revolution itself is costly. Thus, in Figure 11 suppose before the revolution the society grew from A to B; the revolution reduces it to B', from which it grows on the path $B'C$. The cost of revolution depends on the alternatives available. Thus, in Figure 10 suppose that without the revolution the society would have continued at its old rate from say B to C'. Then, the cost of the revolution is shaded triangle $DB'B$. The gains from the revolution consist in the open triangle CDC'. If this goes to infinity the absolute gains are large, but if we discount the future we may easily have a situation in which the revolution was not worth the cost. If a nonrevolutionary acceleration could have been achieved at B where the society following the line ABE, then there are no gains to the revolution whatever, and the cost of the revolution extends into the indefinite future, that is, the society is always worse off at any point in the future because it has had the revolution. The

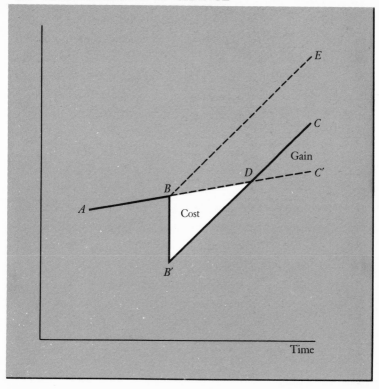

Figure 11. The cost of successful revolution

line *B'C* is always underneath the line *BE*. In any particular historical case, of course, it is often hard to tell whether the gains from a revolution exceed the cost, but certainly the assumption that the gains always exceed the cost is unwarranted. A strong historic case can be made that the gains of revolution rarely exceed the costs and that a nonrevolutionary acceleration is almost always to be preferred to a revolutionary one. Some brief historical examples will illustrate the point.

The French revolution of 1789 is often held up by historians as an example of successful revolution, one which is indeed almost the ideal and the model of subsequent revolutions. It is argued that the revolution was necessary in order to clear away the obsolete feudal and monarchical regime and that without this France would have stagnated or at least developed at a very low rate. The "ifs" of history are very difficult to evaluate. Nevertheless, a strong case can be made that the French revolution was an actual hindrance to French development and that in a sense France has only just recovered from it after close to two hundred years. The revolutionary dialectic in France easily turned into a nationalist dialectic and set France on a road of military expansion which proved enormously costly in diverting her energy from internal developments. Napoleon was costly; Louis Philippe was costly; and the military adventurism of the Third Republic was almost equally costly. The French rate of economic development over this whole period is probably not much above 1 percent per annum, and France, which had easily been the richest and most powerful country in Europe in the eighteenth century, lost the economic leadership of Europe to Germany, which had an acceleration rather than a revolution around 1870.

The American revolution is a more difficult case because it was so cheap. Its cost in terms of actual resources employed was small, and even in terms of refugees, which are one of the principle products of revolution, the cost was not more than about 1 percent of the population. It is quite likely, therefore, that the American revolution is the classic example of a low-cost high-return revolution and that it may be credited with part of the acceleration which followed it. Even here, however, there is some doubt. The real acceleration in American development did not begin until at least a generation after the revolution, and even though the political institutions which were set up by the revolution unquestionably favored development, the development of the nonrevolutionary British Commonwealth societies such as Canada and Australia, considering certain natural disadvantages which they have, has not been very far behind.

The Russian revolution is a much clearer example of a very high-cost revolution, perhaps the highest-cost revolution known to date. It took more than thirty years for real wages in Russia to recover to the 1913 level. It took even longer for per capita income to recover. These losses arose directly out of the revolutionary philosophy of Lenin and Stalin. One sometimes thinks that it is those who have created the most human suffering who are most lauded as heroes. Certainly Lenin and Napoleon were good examples of this. If those who came to power in the Soviet Union had been inspired by developmental instead of dialectical philosophy, and if Russia had had something like the Meiji Restoration in 1917 instead of a revolutionary overthrow, it would probably be much better off today than it is now. It is doubtful even whether the Russian revolution as such produced much in the way of acceleration. Development was proceeding fairly rapidly before 1913, and the rapid growth which has been achieved in recent years have been due more to a relaxation of the revolutionary spirit and should not be credited to the revolution itself.

As we look around the world today, it is hard to avoid the impression that revolutions are becoming more costly all the time, and the case for them gets less and less convincing. It is hard to tell whether the Chinese revolution will turn out to have a higher cost than the Russian revolution; it may indeed turn out to be an example of a fairly low-cost revolution, even though the disaster of the "great leap forward" suggests that all the costs are not yet in. Certainly, if a revolution leads the Chinese in the direction of Napoleonism and racism, as it seems to be doing, the cost indeed will be high. In Indonesia and Cuba, we see examples of extremely high-cost revolutions. These are revolutions which have not, up to now, been accompanied by any acceleration but rather by deceleration. The situation in Indonesia indeed can almost be represented by

Figure 12, where a very slow and unsatisfactory rate of development before the revolution from A to B has been followed by an actual decline from B' to C, though there has been some recovery. Under these circumstances, the cost of revolution is truly enormous. There is real danger, I think, that Cuba will follow the same pattern, and even if at some

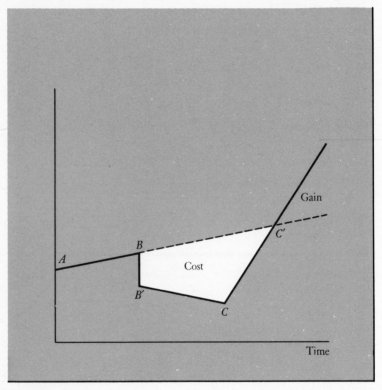

Figure 12. The cost of unsuccessful revolution

future date there is an acceleration, shall we say from C to C', the cost of the revolution is so great as to make it unlikely that any gain from it will be justified.

While one cannot say, therefore, that revolution is never justified, one can say with some confidence that revolutionism is likely to lead to a proliferation of costly and unjustified revolutions. The developmental philosophy, while not ruling out the possibility of desirable revolutions, will put its stress on accelerations rather than revolutions, and especially on ways in which accelerations can be achieved without revolution. Of these perhaps the classic example is the Meiji acceleration in Japan, achieved, it is true, at the cost of a small internal rebellion but almost the classic example of low-cost highly productive acceleration. If we can turn revolutionists into accelerationists, the world will have a much better chance for rapid development and for achieving the great transition through which we are now passing.

It is one thing to see what needs to be done and quite another thing to know how to do it, although seeing what needs to be done certainly is an important first step. The problem of the response to dialectical threat is perhaps the most difficult, and the most unsolved problem which the human race faces. The easy and obvious pattern is for threat to produce counterthreat, and this sets off the dialectical process and opens a Pandora's box of arms races, wars, revolutions, counterrevolutions, riots, suppression, concentration camps, police brutality, and so on. On the other hand, when faced with a situation which seems intolerable and insoluble by any other means, people do and will resort to threat. We see this in a wide variety of situations in the world today. Student protest, for instance, is a worldwide phenomenon in both socialist and capitalist countries. It develops partially because it is easy for young people to be affected by dialectical and revolutionary ideologies which provide legitimation for their hatred of the old who push them around. Furthermore, a revolutionary ideology when it is deeply internalized produces a "heroic" ethic which is careless of personal welfare, despises cost-benefit analysis, and provides a legitimation for a nihilistic destructiveness. A few dedicated individuals of this type can exercise an enormous influence and do a great deal of damage. The negative productivity of human action in destruction can easily be much greater than it is in construction. A boy with a single match can burn down a whole town which took generations to build.

Ordinarily we have strong defenses against this destructiveness, otherwise the human experiment would have ended long ago. All the dialectical forces of wars and revolutions have not prevented the building of cities, the growth of knowledge, and the construction of human institutions and organizations.

Student rebellion is not just a matter of a few misguided leaders. It would not develop at all unless large numbers of students had strong feelings of helplessness in the face of legitimate discontents. Insofar as students themselves are exposed to a threat system, a good deal of their reaction can be interpreted as counterthreat, which in turn creates further counterthreats from those in authority in the shape of suspensions, expulsions, bringing in the police, and so on. The stakes in this matter are very high and may be nothing less than the survival of the human enterprise, for if we cannot legitimate the transmission of knowledge from one generation to the next, the process of social evolution will come to an abrupt end. It is not inconceivable that a dialectical conflict between the generations could have such an effect, although this seems unlikely, if only because of the nondialectical impact of the aging process. Youth, after all, is the one thing that we know has no future, though it sometimes upsets young people if you tell them this. If one generation of young people win the war against the old and their victory sticks, they will certainly live to regret it.

I am not arguing that threats are always destructive or that confrontations accomplish nothing. The attempt on the part of certain groups of students to develop a threat system against teachers and administrations has certainly called attention to problems which have been neglected before, and under some circumstances this has produced desirable reforms. One thinks especially of the reforms of the French universities which seem to have developed as a result of the upheavals of the summer of 1968. The student problem is another illustration of the central proposition of this essay which is that dialectical confrontations are most likely to be fruitful if they take place within a framework of integrative, noncoercive, nonthreatening, and nondialectical relationships. Where, for instance, the academic community is lively and vigorous, it can usually respond to dialectical confrontation creatively in a way that will improve its organization and structure. Where, however, the community itself is weak, dialectical confrontation can easily destroy it to the mutual disadvantage of all sides. Just what it is that makes a community strong or weak, academic or otherwise, however, we still understand imperfectly. The subtle processes by which trust, confidence, respect, and affection are built up among human beings has received very little explicit investigation, at the hands of either philosophers or social scientists. It is much easier to play Cowboys and Indians, which is the ideal literary form of the dialectical process, than it is to knit together the slowly growing tendrils of a community.

Concepts of power

In the last few years the concept of group power has become remarkably salient. Black power, brown power, student power, and now, woman power have become highly charged and meaningful symbols. These concepts should be examined in the light of the principles in this essay. What we are facing is the development of self-consciousness among groups of people who feel that in the past they have lived passively under a threat system which has denied them certain privileges and who now see themselves as establishing their identity as equal members of a society by developing a system of counterthreats. Some of these may lie within the traditional legitimate framework of the system, such as political, economic, and intellectual activity. There are many suggestions, however, that the threats will go beyond this in the direction of civil disobedience and ultimately perhaps to violence.

One can see the attractiveness of the "power" slogan to those who have an acute sense of suffering from powerlessness. In that political developmental process in which an increasingly large proportion of the total population is brought into active participation in the essential decision-making processes of society, the increase in power of the previously powerless is clearly a developmental step. On the other hand, a movement of this kind can also easily slip over into malign conflicts which makes everybody worse off and then can be antidevelopmental even to the point of producing disastrous defeats, disillusionments, and setbacks. Power in the sense of Black power or student power may mean more active participation in the political process, more attention to the kind of productivity which gives real economic power, or to the behavior which leads to integrative power, that is, closer ties of sympathy, understanding, and affection within the total community. The danger is that these other forms of power will not be perceived as realities and that, hence, the rhetoric of the movement will lean more and more in the direction of threat power, that is, the attempt to gain values for themselves by threatening to destroy the values of others. The danger here is that for the poor, the oppressed, and the impotent, the power to make trouble is often the only power that they seem to have and in the absence of any other alternatives it may be too much to ask people not to use it, or at least not the threaten to use it. One of the ways to meet a situation of this kind, therefore, is to expand other areas of power so that the power to be a nuisance is not the only one. Unfortunately, it is not easy to persuade the powerful to relinquish power even when it is to their ultimate advantage.

Perhaps the greatest danger of the rhetoric of power is that it leads to an overestimate of the amount of power which is actually possessed. In the case of the use of threat power, this is particularly dangerous and can lead to disaster. In invoking the threat system one should always be careful of two possibilities. The first is that one may not have the capability of carrying out the threats which are implied. This is why the threat of a general strike has rarely been very effective. Student leaders, likewise, may have dreams of the whole campus in revolt, but what they actually get are small groups of militants who are perceived as troublemakers and all too easily disposed of. The other thing which must be estimated by any users of threat power is the probability of counterthreat being brought up against it. Very often these counterthreats are latent. If a system of threat and submission to threat is working well, indeed, the threats are hardly apparent at all, because the submission is so complete. The threat system, for instance, implied in the tax structure is very rarely brought into play, and most people probably pay their taxes without even thinking about the threat system. It is easy to underestimate the magnitude and effectiveness of the counterthreat system of established authority before it is challenged. Challenge, therefore, often results in disaster for the challenger as well as some cost to the authorities challenged. A revolution that does not succeed is very costly to everybody, and the probability of the success of revolution is not increasing. The movement of modern technology seems to give considerable advantage to established authority, even though we see a possible exception to this principle in the case of Vietnam.

Vietnam is a dialectical tragedy which illustrates all too vividly the tendency of dialectical processes to go beyond the point where they are constructive and to become appallingly costly. The war in Vietnam began as a kind of domestic Vietnamese "American revolution" against the French for national independence, which in the short run was successful. The new country, however, fell apart into civil war much more rapidly than did the United States. The communists sought a dialectical victory by increasing the level of violence through selective assassination. This brought the United States increasingly into the picture, its decision-makers traumatized by the Munich experience of 1938 in their youth and having learned there a lesson which might not be applicable at all in Vietnam. President Johnson, for reasons which are still not clear, escalated the conflict into a major undeclared war. We are beginning to realize that the use of violence has frequently more effect on the user than it has on the victim. Certainly, in the case of Vietnam the bombing in Vietnam has had more impact on the social structure and institutions of the United States than upon those of Vietnam itself. It may well have increased the level of internal violence in the United States, it has destroyed the reputation and power of a president, it has seriously weakened the Democratic Party, and it has widened the generation gap. It would be hard to find a more tragic illustration of the disastrous consequences of dialectical thinking, both at the level of class warfare and international warfare, with the possible exception of the unspeakable tragedies of Nigeria and of the Sudan, where tribal conflicts and civil war have created appalling human suffering and have certainly set back the developmental process for a generation.

The way out of dialectics into a genuinely developmental integrative society is long, hard, dangerous, and precarious. It means crossing a tightrope over a chasm into which it is all too easy to slip. But it seems absurd to start this journey with the theory that tightropes are wonderful and chasms are great things to fall into.

CHAPTER 7

HOW HISTORY MIGHT
BE WRITTEN

In a brief, rather polemical essay, and with the obvious limitations of the author, we cannot expound a grand outline of history along the lines of the developmental interpretation. This would be a task requiring the whole lives of many writers, and it will be a long time before it is accomplished. All we can hope to do in this chapter is to suggest what kind of history might be written by historians whose values and image of the social process correspond in some measure to what is put forward in this volume.

History, as opposed to mere chronology or raw records, is produced by a living subculture of historians, much as an oyster produces a shell. It is the result of an interaction between historians and the record, including the records which have been produced by other historians. History as it is written inevitably reflects the values, interests, ideologies, and theories of the historians, even where these are not explicit or even self-conscious. An underlying question of this whole volume is how can a subculture of historians be produced which writes history that is more "true" than the history written today and in the past.

Truth in history

Just what constitutes truth in history is an epistemological problem of very great difficulty. In an absolute sense, the whole truth can never be known by man, simply because of the epistemological limitations of both his internal and his external environments. Internally, the information processing capacities of the human nervous system, extraordinary and immense as they are, cannot cope with the enormous variety and intricate detail even of the existing historical record. Knowledge, therefore, is always gained at the cost of truth, if by knowledge we mean a workable, operating image of the world which is a guide to human behavior, and if by truth we mean the conceivable maximum which knowledge might attain. The single human organism cannot possibly attain this conceivable maximum of knowledge. Whether any conceivable epistemological organization could attain it is a question we do not have to answer. A question which is legitimate to ask, however, is what processes in society hinder the approach of human images towards truth? Even though we may never know 100 percent truth about the universe and about human history, this does not mean that there is no distinction between history and fiction, between a deliberate attempt to discover truth on the one hand and the flight of creative fancy on the other.

The approach of knowledge towards truth is essentially negative, that is, it moves away from error rather than towards truth, and it proceeds by the elimination of elements in the image that are recognized as not true. Thus, we may be in considerable doubt whether Cain and Abel were historical personages, and some doubt even about the historicity of Moses, but there is no doubt whatever that Mr. Pickwick never existed, except in the imagination of Charles Dickens. This is not to deny that fiction has a "truth" of its own and that it can expand our knowledge in the direction of truth through acquainting us with certain patterns of human life and behavior. But when Virginia grows up she has to learn that there is no Santa Claus as a historical character, although as a symbol he may have significance.

Historians, then, are a group of people engaged in the writing of nonfiction, and we have a right to ask how this activity can be organized in such a way as to detect fiction and differentiate it from history. A great deal of what purports to be history is in fact historical fiction. If it is recognized as such, there is no harm in it. Historical novels, such as *War and Peace,* can enormously expand our appreciation of the significance of a particular phase of history. The fact remains, however, that Napoleon did exist, whereas Pierre, at least as Tolstoy names and describes him, did not.

What we are asking for is not some absolute criterion by which history can be judged—this would be impossible—there is no litmus for historical writing which blushes and detects an untruth. What we are concerned with is the social processes by which history gets written and the components in these processes which lead towards or away from successive approximations of the truth. What we are looking for is elements in the nature of the subculture which produces history and in the nature of the environment of this subculture which may lead to systematic error. Random error tends to be self-corrective. Historical error, which is due to some accidental misreading of the documents or an interpretation which clearly depends on some personal quirk of the historian, is apt to be self-correcting because it pays other historians to detect the error and report it. Systematic error, however, is by its very nature not self-correcting, and therefore may be cumulative. For this reason the detection of systematic error cannot be entrusted to the subculture in which it is imbedded; it can only be detected and exposed through the larger error-detecting capabilities of what might be called the *knowledge culture* in general, that is, that culture which is peculiarly specialized in the production of knowledge and the detection of error.

Error in historical writing

Systematic error in the production of historical writings may come from two groups of sources which can be categorized as *supply* and *demand,* respectively. The suppliers of historical writing are, of course, the historians themselves, and it is to their peculiar characteristics and the characteristics of their subculture in which we must look for systematic error on this side. Historical writing, however, will not ordinarily be produced at all unless there is a demand for it. In rare cases, a historian who has other means of support can write history because he provides his own demand. Usually historical writing is produced because there is a demand for it on the part of other members of society who are not historians. On this side, also, there may be a search for sources of systematic error.

On the supply side, an important source of systematic error is that the raw material of history consists not of events but of records which have been produced by events. These records include fossils, artifacts, such as tools, impressions, buildings, and so on, written records, and in the last hundred years, photographs, soundtracks, and other ways in which the pattern of events impress themselves on the world in a more or less permanent form. Systematic error arises here because the record, as it exists at the time when the historian is working, is a function of the durability of the items which constitute the record, and durability is not necessarily related to significance. Indeed, we may postulate that, for any given cluster of events and states of the world in the past, there is a *preservation ratio,* that is, the ratio of existing records to the activity and conditions to which the record refers. Historians have a natural bias towards the record itself, and this may introduce systematic error simply because the durability of the record is not necessarily related to the significance of the event or the condition which produced it in the first place.

We face the problem of the preservation ratio in the interpretation of all records in the past. Paleontology is always in danger of being biased by the fact that the records which remain in the shape of fossils are bound to be a selective, biased sample of the total ecological system which produced the fossils. Consequently, animals that lived in swamps and left footprints in mud or that produced calcareous shells or skeletons as part of their body structure are much more likely to leave traces in the record than animals that lived in deserts or in rushing mountain streams or that had soft body structures. We face the same problem in the archeological record. People who built structures of brick or stone are more likely to appear in the record than people who built structures of wood or reeds. The same problem applies to the record of communication. Speech, until the last few decades, left no records at all, unless it was transcribed into some form of writing. The written record, however, is a grossly distorted sample of the total volume of human communication. For this reason, some of the most important processes in cultural evolution, such as the development of language, are virtually inaccessible to us, because they left no record on the environment. Hardly anything is less permanent than a sound wave. For the same reason, tools and physical artifacts, such as pottery and metal objects, are well represented in the record, whereas social inventions often leave no direct impression and have to be deduced from changes in artifacts.

One of the functions of those who deal with the record is to improve it, and this goes on all the time through new discoveries, both archeological and literary. Because of the activities of archeologists and literary researchers who have increased the totality of the record on which our judgment has to be based, man's image of his own past today is vastly richer and more accurate than the image which man had of his own past two hundred years ago. Furthermore, there is always, the exciting possibility that new records of great significance may be discovered which may radically alter our image of the past. Historians are indeed aware of this, and the observation that our image of the past undergoes constant change is commonplace. However, the very fact that our image of the past can change under the impact of new records suggests that it may be very far from the truth.

The problem of how to interpret an essentially biased sample, especially where the nature of the bias itself is only imperfectly known, is one that has not received much attention from the theorists of knowledge. It may be that the heavy concentration of statistical theory and the theory of science generally on the experimental sciences may be a source of systematic error. In the experimental sciences in a real sense the record is created by the scientist himself; he is dealing with patterns in the structure of the universe which are essentially repeatable at his will. History, is not repeatable, even though it does exhibit regularity in pattern. It contains strong random elements which make the detection of the underlying pattern very difficult. The processes by which people come to occupy powerful roles almost always have strong random elements in them, and, while the role does to a considerable extent determine the behavior of the occupant, the nature of the occupant also has considerable effect on his own behavior and on the nature of the role itself.

Thus, under the hereditary principle, the accidents of genetics and of personal experience may have a large impact in determining the character of the king who occupies the role simply because he is his father's son. There are, indeed, nonrandom patterns in hereditary succession. The probability that the son of a good king will be a bad one is indeed quite high, but the patterns are constantly masked by the random elements. Similarly, the rise of charismatic individuals who create new roles for themselves and new role structures for others has a strong random element in it, simply because these individuals are so rare. One can hardly doubt that the history of the world would have been substantially different in detail at least if individuals like Buddha, Jesus, or Mohammed, or, on the other side, Alexander, Napoleon, and Hitler had died in infancy. Evolutionary potential in society, as well as in the biological world, is created by improbable events, such as the coming together of a group of people who exercise strong reinforcement on each other, or the development of a succession of events each of which is regarded as somewhat improbable so that the actors in these events acquire a reputation for the miraculous which may afterwards be self-reinforcing.

The regularities of history are essentially probabilistic in nature, and probabilistic regularities are hard to demonstrate. If knowledge grows mainly by the detection of error, how would we detect the error in a prediction that had a 50 percent probability? If a meteorologist predicts a 50 percent chance of rain tomorrow, how can he be disproved? Whatever happens he is right.

Systems with strong random elements in them are always subject to superstition, that is, to the perception of order where in fact there is none, and history is no exception to this rule. It is striking, indeed, that those who have to make historical decisions are remarkably subject to superstition and to making decisions in the light of a perceived orderliness which does not really exist. They attempt to argue by analogy with situations with which they may have been familiar in the past, often when these analogies are completely false.

In addition to these intrinsic difficulties faced by the writers of history we find additional sources of systematic bias in the character of the subculture of historians themselves. In fact, a great deal of human history has been written with the objective of glorifying and supporting the particular ideology of the nation or culture to which the historian belongs. This comes about for reasons both on the side of supply and on the side of demand. In the past, the market for history has consisted largely of those who wish to perpetuate a particular religion, nation, ideology, or social system by transmitting a special image of the past to the minds of the young. The principal market for historians is the educational system, and educational systems are almost universally designed—not altogether unreasonably—to transmit the culture which supports them.

Furthermore, the willingness of historians to supply historical writings for the glorification of the cultures to which they belong is not merely a mercenary matter. It is true that the rewards of conforming historians are usually much larger than those of nonconforming historians and this has some impact. The major element of the situation, however, is that historians usually belong to the culture which they are glorifying, and they, therefore, have a supply of glorification as well as of history. It is not surprising that Russian historians glorify Russia, simply because they are Russians and to glorify Russia is to glorify themselves, that is, to create a more satisfactory image of themselves as Russians. Similarly, American historians glorify America, British historians, Britain, and so on. The only check on this source of error is the development of a world subculture of historians which is professionally oriented. We certainly see the beginnings of this. The fact that historians can collaborate, even though with great difficulty, on a UNESCO history of the world is a straw in the wind. The fact that historians of certain countries, for instance, of Scandinavia, have undertaken to write common histories of their respective societies is also an important indication. Nevertheless, we still find that the history of the Hundred Years' War looks very different in French and in English, that the history of the American Civil War looks different as it is taught in New England or in Georgia, and even the history of the War of 1812 looks very different on the two sides of the Canadian-American border. Thus, because historians tend to belong to their national subcultures rather than to a universal, professional, or scientific subculture, we find forces not only on the side of demand but also very strongly on the side of supply which tend to perpetuate what might be called *special history,* that is history written from the point of view of a particular segment of the human race and history, furthermore, which is designed to glorify some particular segment, usually at the expense of other segments.

The improvement of history must begin with the recognition of the existence of systematic bias, for without this obviously no resources will be put into eliminating it. I may have almost seemed to have demonstrated a nonexistence theorem about history, that both the intrinsic difficulties of the operation and the cultural difficulties which beset its practitioners are so severe that it will certainly not be absurd to despair of even finding a process by which truth might be approximated. Despair, however, is such a useless human emotion that even a false hope may be preferred to a well-founded despair, and the hope of a better history certainly cannot be proved false.

Effect of technology

On what might be called the technical side of record col-
lecting and discovery and the interpretation of the record,
technology surely is on the side of hope. It is not only that
the technology of discovering the record improves all the
time, as witnessed, for instance, in the development of radio-
active dating which is able to exploit aspects of the record
which have never been exploited before. On the side of the
interpretation of the record and the massive problem of
information processing which it presents, simply because of
its enormous size and variety, the development of the
computer also offers considerable hope. The one comparative advantage of the computer is memory and recall. By
means of computers it is now possible both to store and to
process a sheer volume of data orders of magnitude beyond
what the individual human mind can process and store.
It is theoretically conceivable at least that we might build a
computer which would store the whole known record of
the past that is available to mankind. Memory, of course, is
not the same thing as intelligence, and computers have very
little comparative advantage in intelligence, that is, in evaluation, especially evaluation of evaluations and in assessing
significance. One can hope, however, that the man-computer
combination could result in the systematic storage and processing of the total record in a way that would permit
emergence of regularities and patterns and the elimination
of "noise" due to random elements on a scale far beyond the
capability of a traditional historian working only with his
own note-aided memory and the very limited and biased
sample of the record which that contains.

Computer-assisted history may still be a generation away
and even when it comes there are very grave dangers in it,
simply because of the cultural biases which are inherent in
man-the-computer, and perhaps even in the computer itself,

for computers, like people, have a culture and a cultural prejudice in favor of what they are able to do. Nevertheless, it does not seem unreasonable to hope that the enormous expansion of mankind's information-processing facilities which the computer revolution has achieved will in the fairly near future be applied to the problem of how to abstract history out of the record. The record, and this is worth saying twice, is not the same thing as history. History is knowledge which is gained by the orderly elimination of information from the record. The possibilities for putting more order into this elimination process, however, which the computer has opened up, are so great that it seems ungrateful not to be hopeful.

The other problem, that presented by the nature of the subculture of historians, may be more intractible. Nevertheless, it is not absurd to put forward a small amount of hope even here. The problem is how to develop a subculture of historians which will put a high value on what might be called *general history,* as opposed to *special history.* General history would be history written from the point of view of the human race as a whole and from the point of view of what might be called the *human identity* and *mankind values.* Whether it should be concerned with glorification at all is an interesting and difficult point about which there may be some legitimate choices. There is perhaps a tendency to think of general history as being necessarily antiseptic and neutral, non-affective in tone. This does not have to be so. It is possible to visualize a general history which would glorify the human race and the human enterprise as such and which would be a powerful instrument in creating the human identity and a sense of the majesty and splendor, the terror and the bliss of the whole human enterprise. This perhaps is the task of poetry rather than that of history, but I would not want to exclude the poet-historian who, with his feet firmly standing on the rock of a carefully interpreted record, inspires man to lift his head from his daily drudgeries to catch a vision of himself as an actor, however humble, in the majestic drama of the human race as it is spread out like a great banner through time and space.

The time perhaps is not yet ripe for general history and still less perhaps for general poetic history, simply because the culture which could produce it has not yet been established. The human identity and mankind values are everywhere subordinated to special and particular identities and values, whether national, religious, ideological, or class. Under such circumstances, all that can be expected of historians is special history, written to glorify their particular segment of the human race, simply because at the present moment the human identity is considered everywhere to be unpatriotic, irreligious and immoral, and only a saint can dare to aspire to it. Saints, however, are a great rarity, perhaps rightly so, in a subculture of historians.

Nevertheless, we do see the beginnings of the human identity and mankind values in what I have elsewhere called the *superculture* of science and science-based technology. We see this most clearly in the natural sciences, where physics and chemistry are virtually universal subcultures. The periodic table of the elements, for instance, is taught in every chemistry classroom, whether in Peking, Moscow, Rome, New York, or Delhi. There is no such thing as Communist chemistry or Catholic chemistry, American chemistry, or Russian chemistry, and hydrogen is hydrogen the world over. As far as I know, there is not even any lingering outpost where the phlogiston theory is still taught. The power of truth, when it is exerted, is all-conquering. The biological sciences are not in very different condition, although here we do have a little more trouble with the local folk cultures, for instance, in the antievolution laws of Tennessee or in the Lysenko controversy of the Soviet Union. By now, however, the gene is as universal a concept as hydrogen. In the social sciences, we have more diversity representing the fact that they are a little closer to ideology and to dialectical processes. Even here, however, there is a remarkable degree of universality. When it comes to the technical economics, for instance, of input-output analysis, linear programming, or even the role of the price system, there is not very much difference between economics as it is practiced in socialist and in capitalist countries. In the Soviet Union, one may have to find the economics in the mathematics departments rather than in the economics departments, which is more likely to be devoted to a secular theology, but at the technical level at any rate economics is getting to be as universal as chemistry.

Effect of humanities

Even when we come to the field of the humanities, the last fifty years or so have seen remarkable universalization. There is, for instance, an international style in architecture which might be described unkindly as the shoe-box school but which exhibits an extraordinary universality. Even the socialist countries now have succumbed to it, whereas twenty years ago they were the last bastions of victorian and bourgeois pompousness, as in the style which can only deserve the name of "Stalin grotesque." Now, however, all airports look like the same airport, whether they are in Wichita, Prague, Tokyo, or Nairobi. We have also witnessed in the last fifty years a remarkable universalization of all the arts. The Beatles play the Indian sitar and are both enjoyed and imitated in Japan. Abstract art is now virtually universal, except in the socialist countries, where with some exceptions it has had to go underground, and the official art is socialist realism which is remarkably hard to distinguish from bourgeois realism.

This expansion of the world culture of art is by no means a mere cultural imperialism of the West. The "world style," as it seems to be developing, certainly owes as much to African sculpture, to Indian ragas, to Japanese painting and architecture, as to the "classical" European tradition. In many ways, the classical European tradition has come to an end. Not even banks or socialist states, those prime repositories of conservatism, build Grecian temples any more or adorn them with classical sculpture. If, indeed, there is a cultural imperialism in the arts, it is the imperialism of what used to be regarded as primitive, but now is regarded as authentic.

This "mondialization" of culture is seen perhaps most clearly in the universities, where even in the last generation there has been a remarkable disappearance of the exotic and a move towards a curriculum which is based on the world society. When I look back on the Oxford of my undergraduate years in the late 1920's, it seems like an astonishingly parochial institution. "Greats," the traditionally high status curriculum, was still Greek, Latin, and Classical History. If Arabic, Sanskrit, Chinese, Japanese, Urdu, Hindi, Telegu, or Swahili were taught at all, anybody who bothered to learn them would have been regarded as a remarkable oddball. In the great universities today, students still learn Latin and Greek, but just as many probably learn Arabic, Chinese, Japanese, Hindi, and so on. The sense that one had at Oxford forty years ago that there was only one main stream of human history coming out of Egypt, Israel, and Babylon through Greece and Rome has now quite disappeared, and we see what used to be called *classics* as merely one tradition out of many.

In spite of all these developments, the world society is still some way off. The fact that the world war industry, as measured by the total of world monetary budgets, was some 200 billion dollars in 1969, about equal to the total income of the poorest half of the human race, suggests that the world society is still in a very primitive state and is deeply threatened by internal schisms. The world war industry is a symbol of the deep mistrusts and malevolences which still characterize a very large proportion of the human race. Furthermore, as the "superculture" develops momentum, we may quite legitimately find reactions against it and deliberate attempts to preserve the peculiarities and the special features of the different cultures of mankind. A great deal of revolutionary zeal, for instance, is directed not so much against particular oppressors and exploiters as such, but against the enormous dynamic impetus of the world economy and the superculture as it is expressed, for instance, in the international corporations. China is an extreme example of the attempt of a society to isolate itself completely from the ongoing world culture. Burma is another country which has gone into what might almost be called *Tokugawa shock,* as Japan did in the period of the Tokugawa withdrawal from the world. It is not surprising, therefore, to find that historians do not participate in the world culture in the way that scientists, social scientists, and even artists do. Until, however, there is a universal subculture of historians, there cannot be a truly universal history.

The problem, indeed, may now lie more on the side of supply than on the side of demand. The great universities, and even to a considerable extent the smaller colleges, are providing an increasing market for a genuinely universal history, and there is increased awareness among educators everywhere that a universal history is an essential part of the educational process which is appropriate to the age of space and nuclear energy. The supply, however, presents a real difficulty. The reward structure of the historical profession does not tend to provide it, and the inherent difficulties which we have seen earlier are very great. It is much harder for a historian to separate himself professionally from his own national society than it is, say, for a chemist, who puts on a universal personality when he puts on his white coat and takes it off again when he walks out in his ordinary clothes. Historians have no white coats; they wear their ordinary clothes all the time. It is, therefore, particularly hard for them to dissociate themselves from the national and local culture in which they have grown up. Even those who have dreamed of a universal history, such as Vico in the eighteenth century, Herbert Spencer and Walter Bagehot in the nineteenth century, and Arnold Toynbee in the twentieth century, could not liberate themselves from their essentially West European, Christian backgrounds and, indeed, could not reasonably be expected to be so liberated. Our local and special identities are facts of the social system which we have to acknowledge and with which we have to come to terms. Thus, even while I am myself an ecumenist, impatient of passports and visas and the artificial restrictions which divide men from one another and yearn for a truly human identity which will transcend all others, I have to recognize also that I am inescapably a Westerner, raised in a Protestant, Christian, English-speaking, Anglo-American environment, from which I cannot escape and from which in many ways I do not wish to escape. Even if I were a historian, therefore, and had the time and the talent to do the task, I would be unfitted by my education and culture to write the kind of universal history which I believe to be possible.

Nevertheless, it is possible to suggest what it is that one cannot do yet at the same time to indicate what might be the scope and the flavor of a truly universal history. It would begin with biological evolution, at least with the evolution of the human organism, little as we know about this. All we do know is that some time in the past, within the period from two million to half a million years ago, a creature appeared on the face of this planet essentially similar biologically to man as we know him today. The evidence suggests that there has been very little biological development of mankind for a long time, at least as far as the human genetic structure is concerned. Whether the human gene pool today is substantially different in its proportions from what it was ten thousand or a hundred years ago, we may perhaps never know. What is certain is that these changes are much smaller than the changes that occurred within the structure of the human nervous system itself through the process of human learning and that by and large human history is essentially a history of human learning. The physiology of human history takes the form mainly of a history of nutrition and of disease. These, however, are essentially environmental rather than genetic in character, although changes in the human gene pool cannot be ruled out a priori as insignificant.

The would-be universal historian is always tempted to divide history into stages. This attempt is by no means absurd, as history, even the history of biological evolution, is characterized by periods of relative stability in the structure of species, divided by periods of relatively rapid change. The great river of evolutionary development, as it were, is not a continuous flow through time, but can be broken up roughly into pools, which represent stages, and rapids or waterfalls, which represent revolutionary transitions. The pattern is so attractive and so valuable from the point of view of exposition that there is real danger of imposing it on the reality which represents a much more continuous flow. It is, indeed, the principal argument of this volume that the revolutionary changes are incidents imposed on the larger pattern of development and play a relatively small role in creating the dynamics of the developmental pattern. The problem noted earlier of the preservation ratio is of particular importance here because the long, slow, nondialectical processes frequently do not leave residues, whereas more dramatic transitions may often leave a more salient record.

Thus, even if we take what seems to be the most generally

accepted system of stages today, the sequence paleolithic, to neolithic, to civilization, and to the developed society, though the periods of transition seem to be very short by comparison with the periods of stability, this may be more a part of the nature of the record than of the reality. Thus, in the seemingly almost endless equilibruim of the paleo-lithic, it seems plausible to speculate that man was con-stantly occupied in developing language and that it was only when language was fully developed to the point where abstract ideas could be expressed that the great in-ventions of agriculture and domestication of animals and plants could take place and be transmitted. What seems like a very dramatic change, then, about ten thousand years ago might perhaps be viewed as a culmination of a very long learning process which only at that moment broke through to have an impact on artifacts and residues.

Similarly, the so-called urban revolution and the transi-tion to civilization now seems not to have been as sudden as at first believed, but was foreshadowed by urban experi-ments like Jericho and by the development of metallurgy and international trade, so that the transition may appear from the records to be more dramatic than it actually was. We see the same phenomenon in the so-called industrial revolution and the breakthrough into science and science-based technology. It is now clear that the scientific revolu-tion was prepared by a long process of gradual technical change and improvement which began in Western Europe almost from the date of the fall of Rome. I have argued, indeed, that what has been called the Industrial Revolution in England in the eighteenth century was merely the cul-mination of a long process of medieval development and was in fact prescientific. The spinning jenny was intrinsically no more complex than the medieval clock and did not em-body any new mechanical principles. The printing press was an adaptation of the long development of the wine

press and even the steam engine grew out of a folk technology rather than out of pure science. It may have owed
something to Boyle's Law, but it certainly owed nothing to
the science of thermodynamics which was not developed
until almost a hundred years after the steam engine. Thermodynamics, indeed (Carnot published in 1824), owed
much more to the steam engine than the steam engine did
to thermodynamics. About the middle of the nineteenth
century we can detect a transition into the science-based
industries. The chemical industry, for instance, would have
been impossible without Dalton and Kekulé. The electrical
industry would not have developed without Faraday and
Clerk-Maxwell, and the nuclear industry could not have
developed without Rutherford, Einstein, and Bohr. No
amount of watching kettles could have split the atom. The
full effect of this transition may not be felt till many centuries in the future. But even this can be seen as a passing
of a threshold as a result of a very long buildup of human
knowledge and institutions.

The concept of stages becomes of less and less value as we
move to shorter periods and finer distinctions. The transition both into and out of feudalism, for instance, in Europe
was so gradual that it is impossible to say where it begins
or ends as a stage. The problem of stages is closely related
to that of comparative classifications of societies. Was pre-
Tokugawa Japanese society "feudal" or is this an illegitimate
extension of the term? The fact is that any society as it
exists at a given moment of time is a complex aggregation
of elements some of them reinforcing each other and some
of them contradictory. It is the elements rather than the
society that change. Though there may be some clustering
of elements which enable different types of society to be
named and classified, these names and classifications represent largely arbitrary divisions of what is really an *n*-dimen-
sional continuum. One hopes, therefore, that the universal

history will be able to follow these continuous strands in human development rather than maintain the fiction that the fabric of one stage is suddenly transformed into a different fabric of another stage. This is not to deny, of course, that there are breaks in the fabric of history. The disasters —natural or man-made—which overthrew Knossus or Jerusalem, Babylon or Chichen Itza do bring a complex pattern to an end. These real rips in the fabric, however, are quite rare, and they often represent merely a displacement of the pattern, as the seat of empire is moved to a new locality or to a different group of powerful role occupants. Even traditional historical language here is often misleading. Rome did not "fall," it withered away over a thousand years, and the final fall of Constantinople to the Turks in 1453 was only the tiniest rip in the fabric, not much more significant than thousands of others.

To try to interpret history as a succession of dominant classes, as the Marxists do, is no more realistic than to think of it as a succession of stages. It is true that the development of societies in which there is a dominant and a dominated group is a phenomenon so common as to be almost universal, and it is also particularly characteristic of the rise of civilization and the urban revolution. The relatively classless society of the neolithic village is perhaps reflected in the myths of the Golden Ages, Garden of Eden, Primitive Communism and the like. The urban revolution and the invention of civilization in a real sense represents a "fall," simply because it is a product of the development of an organized threat system. Nevertheless the forms which domination has taken are legion, just as there are innumerable facets of justification and legitimation for a class structure. Even in an institution like slavery, there is a wide spectrum of different social forms between extremes of the pure chattel slavery of the anti-bellum American South and the free labor market. Even the three-fold division of the aristocracy, bourgeoisie, and the working class is in many societies a purely linguistic categorization which hides immense complexity and indeed continuity of the structure. The effort which many societies have felt obliged to put into symbolizing and maintaining class distinctions in matters of title, dress, sumptuary legislation, and so on is an indication of the essential artificiality and erodibility of these categories. In every society an enormous process of social erosion is continually going on. Even in South Africa today, for instance, apartheid is continually being eroded at the edges by sheer economic development, as in medieval Europe the "apartheid" policies of the aristocracy were eroded by inflation, by increasing wealth of the merchant group, by war, and by marriage. Even interaction of classes, which is a shorthand for the dynamics of the structure of dominance within the society, is an immensely complex n-dimensional pattern, and over large stretches of history is more subject to nondialectical than to dialectical processes. One of the most fascinating tasks of a true universal history, indeed, would be precisely the one which is proposed in this volume that of identifying the dialectical and the nondialectical processes in human history and assessing their relative value and importance in the total picture of social dynamics and change. The task is by no means easy and in part may be impossible, simply because of the losses in the record and the difficulties of measuring and detecting the great, long, continuous, nondialectical changes. Nevertheless, if the spirit of this task can inspire future historians, one hopes that the history that will be written will gain both in interest and in significance and will approach more closely to the elusive truth.

JAPAN: A CASE STUDY

I t is only with the greatest hesitation that I venture to say anything about Japan. I lived in Japan a little less than a year in 1963–64. This was time enough to acquire a smattering of knowledge but also time enough to realize the depth of my ignorance. Japan is a society of great complexity and subtlety. The best word I can think of to describe it is that it is a mosaic society, in the sense that it is composed of numerous colorful pieces all of which together form, in some mysterious way, a pattern. If I may be permitted to play on words, it is the least Mosaic of all societies, participating hardly at all in that great stream of history which comes down from Mt. Sinai—until the last one hundred years.

Influence of Marxism

We may, perhaps, invoke both the elements mentioned above to explain in part one of the paradoxes of Japanese society—the extraordinary fascination which Marxism seems to exercise on the Japanese mind, especially the Japanese intellectual. The intricate quality of the society and the fact that it is extremely hard to understand, even for the Japanese, gives a simplified explanation like Marxism a certain appeal, even if the explanation does not conform closely to reality. Man seems to have a strong dislike for randomness and disorder, even to the point, as we saw in an earlier chapter where he will ascribe law or a pattern to a random series. The very intricacy of Japanese society, therefore, creates a certain demand for a simplified abstract picture, and for some minds especially, the spectacle of so much complexity and the pattern of fragmentation is almost unbearable. It may even be that the Judaic quality of Marxist thought meets a need in the Japanese mind which is not felt so deeply in those societies which have long been exposed to Judaic religions, for Marxism has quite properly been called the third great Judaic religion, coming after Christianity and Islam. Its insistence on the reality of history and the importance of time, its view of history as a one-way street with some sort of triumphal arch marking the beginning of the bright Messianic future, its monistic and intolerant interpretation of ultimate reality, its strong distinctions between the good and evil and its insistence that it always knows the difference between them, and its insistence that man and society are subject to law are strong marks of its Jewish origin. In some ways, indeed, Marxism is a more Jewish faith than Christianity. The materialist interpretation of history is more akin to the wrathful judge of the Old Testament than to the loving father of the New.

The influence of Marxism in Japan, therefore, may perhaps be attributed to a certain reaction against a value system based on manners rather than morals and on shame rather than guilt. Marxism in practice lays an enormous stress on the internalization of its moral imperatives, as the purges and the self-incriminations which have characterized so much communist history clearly indicates. This is a long way from the polytheism, tolerance, and externalization of behavior which seems to be characteristic of much of Japanese traditional society. Marxism in Japan, therefore, is part of that whole rejection of the traditional society which followed the first impact of the west in the middle of the nineteenth century and which also resulted in the reintroduction of Christianity.

Another possible explanation, which I put forward with considerable hesitancy, however, is that the appeal of Marxism and especially of dialectical philosophy arises out of the nature of the Japanese family and early childhood experiences. Families which are dominated by an authoritarian father are supposed to produce deeply suppressed resentment in the minds of the children. Marxism is a wonderful way to legitimize this resentment, for it legitimizes hatred and even violence directed against the father figures of those in authority. It is easy to see in Marx's image of the class structure a parallel with the structure of the authoritarian family. As we have seen earlier, there is a certain dialectical process which takes place within the family as the parents age and the children eventually replace the parents in the dominant role, to be replaced in their turn by their own children. To someone raised in an authoritarian family, the dialectical pattern would appear very convincing because it does describe what happens in the family history, and it would be easy to project this on to the total society. It would be an extremely interesting subject for research to try to relate the nature of the family and early childhood training with the prevailing political view of a society. This research has not been done on a large scale, and the theory has no more status than a tentative hypothesis. Man is a complex creature, and one is suspicious of any single or simple interpretation of human behavior.

Even though Marxism has been an important influence in Japan, it has by no means been dominant. In the last hundred years, the dominant philosophy has been what might be called *dialectical nationalism* and this is oddly inconsistent with the sensitivity, tolerance, and strongly non-dialectical character of traditional Japanese culture. The image which Japan created for herself in the world in the last hundred years indeed has been strangely ambiguous. On the one hand, there are cherry blossoms, haiku, and tea ceremony, and the subtle and esthetic qualities of Japanese life. On the other hand, there is the image in the west of a cruel, hard-faced little soldier utterly insensitive to any communication except that of brute force. Reality of course would be much more complex than either of these two images. Nevertheless, these do represent, as it were, the poles of the Japanese experience. It was the dialectical nationalism which saw everything Japanese as good, everything foreign as bad and which could see the world not in terms of problem solving and adjustment but only in terms of conquest, which led Japan to its great disaster. It is tempting indeed to see in the authoritarian family the source of both the dialectical philosophies which have been so influential in Japan. Marxism represents the revolt against the father figure and dialectical nationalism represents a pathological submission to the father figure in the image of the emperor and the transfer of the suppressed resentments from the father figure itself to the foreigner who is outside of the national family.

Paradox of Japanese history

Even though we may explain the influence of dialectical philosophies in Japan by reference to certain elements and structures of the society, nevertheless, a paradox remains, because Japan has one of the least dialectical of all histories. One's first impression is that this is one of the most continuous, nondialectical, nonrevolutionary histories in the whole story of mankind. There was, of course, feudal war, which represents in a sense a dialectical system, there is a rise and fall of dynasties and shogunates, there are periods of rapid change as in the seventh century or nineteenth and twentieth centuries, and there are the periods of relative stagnation. Through all this, however, one is conscious of a quite extraordinary continuity of culture, and one has the impression of a society dominated for two thousand years by long, slow, and continuous change with occasional accelerations.

One sees this most graphically perhaps in art and architecture. It takes an expert to be able to date a piece of Japanese architecture, although there is a long, slow change and development. In Europe a superficial knowledge will enable one to date a building within fifty or a hundred years. There is nothing in Japan like the extraordinary transformation of styles in Europe from Greek and Roman architecture to the Gothic and back again to the Renaissance which looks like a dialectical process written in stone. It is not until the last hundred years that there is any radical change in architectural styles, and this is only because Japan has become enmeshed in a worldwide technological transformation which is in the process of transforming all traditional societies. Even the Meiji Restoration in its economic aspects can be regarded essentially as the mere acceleration of changes which were already under way in the late Tokugawa period. Had it not been indeed for the slow continuous change which went on in spite of the shoguns, all through the Tokugawa period, such as the development of the money economy, the improvement in agricultural techniques, the slow rise in population, the development of large urban centers, and even a gradual introduction of "Dutch Learning",—the European science and technology which crept in through the Dutch merchants "ghetto" at Nagasaki—the rapid development which followed the Meiji Restoration would have been quite impossible.

In 1618 the Tokugawa settlement was a striking example of the successful obsolescence of an internal dialectical process. Japan "enjoyed" stable feudal war for many centuries with a primitive military technology. The loss-of-power gradient was so high as one went away from the local daimyo's castle that it was easy for another center of power to establish itself a relatively short distance away. The introduction of gunpowder and fire arms made this system profoundly unstable. The daimyo lost their viability as independent centers of power. It took a surprisingly short time, hardly more than two generations, after the introduction of firearms, for power to become centralized in the Tokugawa shogunate, which resulted in the abolition of the dialectical process of feudal war. By the middle of the seventeenth century, Japan made the transition from stable internal war to stable internal peace, broken only by occasional short-lived rebellions. In all this history the continuity of the emperor as a symbol, even when he was powerless, introduced one strong nondialectical element into the society, and this undoubtedly played an important role in permitting it to resolve and overcome its internal dialectical processes. The emperor has provided for Japan, as it were, a nondialectical reserve of political resources on which it has been possible to draw on a number of critical occasions, especially in the Meiji Restoration and in the ending of the Second World War. Without this reserve it might have been impossible to transfer power from the Shogunate in 1868 without a disastrous civil war much larger in scale than the Satsuma rebellion. In 1945 the country might have been fought over mile by mile and have suffered division like Germany.

Surplus value

Insofar as the concept of surplus value is an important social reality, of course, it is a useful tool in the interpretation of Japanese as of any other history. We can see very clearly in the feudal period how the excess of production of the food producer beyond his own requirements for maintenance and reproduction were generally taken away from him by the superior threat of the feudal lord and his retainers. In the Tokugawa period the threat system was centralized in the *bakufu,* but the surplus production was still siphoned from the food producer and used deliberately to pension off the samurai and to feed the centrally controlled armed force. Incidently, it also fed the artisans who built Nikko, the citizens of the gay quarters, the inn keepers of the Tokaido, and the creators of the wonderful outpouring of art and poetry which the period produced. In the Meiji Restoration the surplus food-stuffs were still squeezed out of the farmer much as before but instead of being used to feed courtesans and the vast army of unemployed samurai, it was used to feed the students in the new universities and the builders of railroads and steel mills. It is only in the twentieth century that industrial output has become high enough so the farmers can get much in return for the food which he sells.

In all this process the class structure was profoundly unclear, and the Marxist theory of a dialectical succession of classes bears little relation to what actually went on. The Meiji Restoration was not a bourgeois revolution, even though, in a sense, it had this result. The samurai were not eliminated as in the French revolution in a good dialectical fashion, but became bankers, businessmen, and professionals and contributed enormously to the modernization and development of Japan. Japanese history is a history of interpenetration of classes rather than of their succession. At all times, furthermore, the national consciousness, or even local loyalties, has tended to transcend class consciousness. The Japanese political and social landscape, like the landscape of Japanese painting, is suffused with a gentle mistiness which removes all sharp distinctions and makes it almost impossible to locate the place where decisions are made. By contrast, the sharply edged European landscapes and the European political scene reflect a society in which distinctions are clear and battle lines are sharply drawn. Of all systems of social taxonomy, therefore, the Marxist class theory seems the least well adapted to interpret the almost infinite subtlety and complexity of Japan where even interpersonal communication seems to rely not only on formal language but also on a kind of social radar which establishes a widespread understanding of a position without ever clearly stating it.

For Japan, therefore, the popularity of dialectical philosophy both in the form of militant nationalism and in the form of Marxism has had uniformly unfortunate results. It has diverted attention from the reality of the social situation and driven people into decisions which have had disastrous consequences. One sees this particularly in the whole set of decisions which led to the Second World War. There is a myth, which is fairly widespread even outside Japan and is naturally highly popular inside, that Japan was "forced" into the Second World War by economic pressures and the unwillingness of dominant imperial powers, especially England, France, and the United States, to permit it to expand its export industries. There may be a grain of truth in this view, but it is a very small grain indeed. The Japanese economy, it is true, did stagnate somewhat in the 1920's almost entirely as a result of the foolish deflationary policies which seriously hampered domestic investment and restricted domestic consumption. Japan did extremely well economically out of the First World War by staying out of military activity and supplying the combatants, especially, of course, the Allies. By the end of the war Japan had built up a very large reserve of foreign currency through selling her goods to the Allies at inflated prices. After the war in the 1920's she spent these foreign balances for imports at much lower prices. The terms of trade of this whole transaction must have been very favorable. Economically, Japan got very little out of her imperial and expansionist adventures. As it turned out, she lost very heavily, losing all her heavy investment in her colonies. The economic fact, however, is that in the period of military expansion from say 1890 to 1930, the growth of per capita income in Japan was only about 2.3 percent, whereas after the defeat in 1945, the extensive land destruction, the loss of her whole empire, and the return of three million Japanese from overseas, per capita income has been rising at more than 8% per annum. The brutal fact of the modern world is that the way to get rich is to stay home and mind ones own business well. For Japan the economic rate of return on military investment was highly negative.

If Japan had been guided by a different philosophy, more nondialectical in character, she could have done in the Second World War exactly what she had done in the first. She was not really threatened by anybody, as England, France, Russia, and the smaller European countries were threatened by Germany. The United States was in an isolationist, almost "Tokugawa" mood as the neutrality legislation clearly showed, and although President Roosevelt very much wanted to get the United States into the Second World War he was unable to do this until the attack on Pearl Harbor. If, indeed, Japan had not attacked Pearl Harbor, it is doubtful whether the United States would have entered the Second World War at all. Germany would gradually have been exhausted, unconditional surrender would not have been insisted upon, and some sort of peace might have been worked out. As it was, Japan deliberately provoked the sleeping tiger of the United States, the consequence of which we all know.

We need major research on the nature of the learning process by which the rulers and indeed most of the people of Japan came to accept a view of the world power structure which involved them in such disastrous and absolutely unnecessary decisions. In part, of course, we can trace this learning process back to the "black ships" of Admiral Perry and the lesson which they taught that a country with a feudal economy, technology, and weapons was likely to be pushed around in the modern world. This lesson probably had some truth in it. A succession of fairly cheap wars, however, especially the Chinese war of 1895, which yielded a large increase in territory, a colonial empire, and a place in the councils of the great powers taught the lesson that military adventure paid off. The conquest of Manchuria was another extraordinarily cheap exercise of the threat system. Generalizing falsely from this experience, Japan went into China, which turned out to be a military morass. In the meantime, the educational system has propagated a philosophy of dialectical nationalism which eventually stifled criticism and led to the final disaster.

At the other end of the scale, the dialectical aspects of Marxism seem to have led to the virtual impotence of political criticism in Japan. The socialist party, which is still the largest opposition party, is split between the dogmatic Marxists on one hand and the more realistic revisionists on the other. This split created a third party, the Democratic Socialist Party, consisting of people who could not stand the domination of the socialist party by dogmatic Marxists. The labor movement is similarly split. The teacher's union, dominated by a dialectical philosophy, has wasted its energy in a useless class war between the teachers, the ministry of education, and even the parents, which seems to have led to the disappearance of almost all useful discussion and criticism. In the student movement, likewise, the zengakuren has followed a policy derived from an almost purely dialectical philosophy which produced impressive demonstrations in 1960 but virtually no fruitful criticism. As a result, the movement itself is discredited, and its leaders deplore the prevailing student apathy which they did so much to create.

New direction

Japanese development since 1945 not only established a world record for the rate of economic growth, but it is growth in which virtually all sections of society participated. It is an extraordinary example of the success of an essentially nondialectical philosophy. Japan could easily have done otherwise. It could have brooded over its defeat and planned revenge, or it could have sunk inself into the apathy of despair. Instead, it seemed to shake off, almost like casting away an outworn cloak, the philosophy of dialectical nationalism which had brought it so low, and it turned to solving its problems instead of finding someone to blame for them. It cooperated with the conqueror, the cardinal sin of any dialectical philosophy, and as a result it rebuilt its cities, its factories, and its exports, reformed its land tenure, overhauled its tax system, and laid the foundations for one of the most remarkable economic developments of all time. It indulged in few recriminations, settled down in a thoroughly nondialectical way to work hard and saved nearly fifty percent of its income. The American occupation, no doubt, did some foolish things along with some wise ones, but the Japanese put up with them and when the opportunity arose corrected them.

Nevertheless, one cannot look at the present situation without a certain disquiet. The teacher's union has a strong dialectical philosophy and inevitably young minds to which these ideas are presented often find them attractive. There is indeed in dialectical philosophy something which is dramatic, simple, and peculiarly attractive to the young. We see this, for instance, in the popularity of cowboy movies and of the Japanese equivalent, the samurai movie. It is nice to be able to divide the world into good guys and bad guys and to see history as a simple struggle in which righteousness struggles against evil and in which the main problem for the individual is how to find out who are the good guys and join them. The developmental philosophy is more subtle. It is unfriendly to simple solutions and black and white pictures; it stresses what often seems to be a humdrum business of sitting down with people to solve problems; it discourages the striking of noble attitudes; it plays down the desire for victory; it stresses compromise and accommodation, all of which sorely tries the heart and mind of youth, which constantly hankers after the heroic simplicities of struggle. When the teachers, therefore, teach dialectical philosophy, this is likely to raise a whole generation bent on undermining the solid achievements of the developmental process, and in the long run this could turn the country into disastrous internal strife. It could even produce a turn again toward dialectical nationalism, for between the philosophy of class war and the philosophy of international war, there is a thin line and it is easy to pass this divide. Furthermore, the weakness of class as a symbol and as the source of integrative relations means that the passions which are generated by stirring up a class war easily get transferred to a foreign foe.

The fact that so much in the way of political energy and criticism has been wasted in a futile dialectical process may have other unfortunate consequences for the future of

Japan. Because so much political energy and criticism has been wasted, the sort of hard thinking which goes into responsible criticism has not been done. There has been extraordinarily little attempt, for instance, to think out the real implications for foreign policy of the peace clause in the Constitution. Instead, the discussion has taken the barren form of those who want to revise the Constitution, saying "we will" and those in opposition saying "you won't." The absence of responsible criticism here can easily lead to the very process of slipping back into the old nationalism which those who want to preserve the existing constitution quite rightly fear. Similarly, in regard to economic policy, the success of the present policy is to some extent accidental, that is, it has been a matter of good luck as well as good management. The people who determine the economic policy of Japan are certainly not stupid, but they do not have more than a very broad general theory of the working of the economy, and a sudden change of conditions might easily catch them without appropriate measures. The criticism of economic policy, however, being conducted in purely dialectical terms, contributes very little to the understanding of real issues involved.

Japan faces a major economic readjustment some time within the next ten years. An eight percent per annum rate of economic growth cannot and should not be maintained forever. At some time or other the fruits of all this self sacrifice should be enjoyed. Instead of consuming only little over fifty percent of the national product and investing close to forty percent, Japan will have to move to a much higher ratio of consumption and a lower ratio of investment. In order to do this, however, there almost certainly will have to be radical changes in the price structure, in wages, in interest rates, in taxation, and in the financial system. These changes can certainly be achieved nondialectically, especially if there is wide understanding of what needs to be done. Nevertheless, even in an essentially non-dialectical or developmental process, as we have seen, there is frequently an opportunity and indeed a necessity for dialectical processes of a constructive nature. The alternation of the parties in a workable two-party democracy is a process of this kind. It could very well be that a party committed to broader social ideals, to higher levels of consumption, and a wider distribution of income would be the most satisfactory instrument to achieve the kind of adjustment which Japan is going to have to make. At present, unfortunately, one cannot see the socialist party in this role simply because of its domination by an extreme and obsolete dialectical philosophy. A broader-based less ideological party of the left would have a better chance of achieving power and a much better chance of doing something useful with the power once it was achieved.

Here again we see an excellent example of a case in which extreme adherence to a dialectical philosophy at almost all costs is likely to prove costly not only for the people who hold it but also for the whole country. There is here, perhaps, a great opportunity for a few people who hold what might be called a developmental philosophy of the left to develop a genuine and constructive criticism of existing policies and even perhaps eventually a real alternative to the Liberal Democratic Party. It would be quite presumptuous for me as an outsider to suggest how or by whom this might be done.

It is not far fetched to call Japan the first twenty-first-century country. The capacity of the Japanese to learn all that the rest of the world has to teach them and hence to take off into the modern world at an unprecedented rate suggests that what is happening and is likely to happen in Japan has a significance far beyond its local impact. Of all the societies in the world, Japan is most likely to be a model for the future. Unlike the United States, it is crowded and short of natural resources, a characteristic of most of the rest of the world. It has a rich and attractive traditional culture which it has managed to preserve, if not intact, at least in a modified form in the middle of the hurricane of change. It has learned a bitter lesson that in the modern world the nationalistic dialectic (war) and imperialism are disastrous, and we must learn to do without them. It is facing enormous problems of congestion and pollution, and it will face perhaps before any other society the problem of what I have come to call "re-entry," that is, how do we make the transition from rapid development into the more stable "spaceship earth" which we must come to in the future. If the beginning of development is a "takeoff," then development itself is a kind of voyage through social space which must be followed by a re-entry and landing in a new kind of world. Japan has had the most rapid voyage through this social space of development, so it is likely to be one of the first societies which will have to face the problems of re-entry and of establishing a new, high level, much more stable, conservation-minded society. This will require a much more "looped" economy in which the waste products of society, both material and psychological, will have to be re-cycled and used as raw materials in a continuing circular process. Revolutionary and dialectical ideologies make no contribution at all to the solution of this, the most fundamental problem of the future. What is needed is something much more fundamental than revolution, something involving a much greater change in the state of man than a mere change in the distribution of power. It would not surprise me if Japan were the first country to respond to this challenge, and its history therefore may be of enormous importance for the whole of mankind.

INDEX

INDEX

INDEX

INDEX

INDEX